About the Author

Brendan Murphy was born into the Irish diaspora, returning home to Ireland in 1996. He has lived in the Cooley Mountains in Tullaghomeath, high above Carlingford Lough, since 1997. As an international business consultant focusing on leadership, organisational design and transformation, he has worked in many countries and visited more, as an explorer of people and places. His involvement in Ukraine extends back to 1998 and he has unbreakable connections forged through friendship and romance, of the usual kind. Since 17 March (Patrick's Day) 2020, Brendan lived in Irpin and explored Ukraine, until the fateful day Russia attacked.

War in Ukraine: An Irishman's Journey

Brendan Murphy

War in Ukraine: An Irishman's Journey

Olympia Publishers
London

www.olympiapublishers.com

OLYMPIA PAPERBACK EDITION

A CIP catalogue record for this title is
available from the British Library.

ISBN: 978-1-80439-144-0

This is a work of creative nonfiction. The events are portrayed to the
best of the author's memory. While all the stories in this book are
true, some names and identifying details have been changed to
protect the privacy of the people involved.

First Published in 2023

Olympia Publishers
Tallis House
2 Tallis Street
London
EC4Y 0AB

Printed in Great Britain

Dedication

Dedicated to the memory of those who died, to those who are suffering, to the kindness of strangers, my family and my friends. *Spéartha geala agus bóthar ag ardú.*

Acknowledgements

My financial contribution to this book was funded using GoFundMe and I am sincerely grateful to those who donated. The list of those who did so are on my page https://gofund.me/419eb554. I am indebted to, James, at Olympia Publishers, who is the coolest dude, answering my questions in time and with clarity. As well as, Kristina Smith, who guided the book to publication. I am indebted to my sisters and brothers, our parents, Yvonne, Svetlana and Anna, and the many other hands that moulded this difficult clay into some sort of human, far from perfect, I know. I apologise that I am poor material for such kindness, guidance and support. I have no medical or psychological condition to excuse my ways, so put it down to nature and my inability to learn. What's good in me was kneaded by many strong hands. To my neighbours in Irpin, and my neighbours in the mountains above Omeath, thank you. Loneliness is impossible when all you have to do is reach out and touch, and even though I don't, I know you are there. I am there for you also. Four in particular, Nataliya, Pauline, and the unmatchable David and Veronica Smyth, whose Rally School Ireland is without equal. Thank you for your kindness, rare touch. To Oleg, my great good friend, sincere thanks for the things you do. You're a good man. To Sofia… well, you know I love you. That will never change. Find your place, and be happy. If you don't see yourself in this book, that's my fault. But you are there, a watermark in my character. *Na hÉireannaigh agus an Úcránach, ceangailte le stair, carachtar agus anam.*

Foreword

The dangers of russia are evident and undeniable, which is why the capital R is not used in its name. No nation should stand amongst the peoples of the world, having the opinions, behaviours and activities that are now universally known to define the territory called russia.

These dangers are very real, and some of the names in this book have been changed to protect those concerned. Such is the evil and animosity of the russian state that there will never be a day where some of them can be known.

And, in any case, these perfect people are the bedrock of societies, and they don't need the stress of intrusion.

But, in case you are in any doubt, yes, they saved our lives.

Is leatsa an mairimid.

Chapter 1
Ukraine

It was raining hard, bouncing off the car with a solid metallic thud, as I sat in the car park, waiting to meet a client. I was pondering life and the weather in Ireland when the phone rang; a big block of a phone which flipped open when you wanted to use it. Opening it was like working a Rubik's cube.

As I fumbled, I heard a disconnected voice above the plinking sound of the rain. "Hello, hello? Is that Brendan?"

"*Err,* yes, yes, that's me. I'm Brendan."

"Oh, hi, someone at Microsoft gave me your name, we need help. It's our business, it isn't working."

As a business consultant, I get many such calls, but no other has had such an impact on my life as this one.

You see, this was an agency recruiting Ukrainians for the IT and agriculture sectors in Ireland and it was 1997.

Few realise that Ukrainians form part of the bedrock of Ireland's global IT industry, and in fact the world's computer industry, starting with Professor Kateryna Yushchenko, based in Kyiv.

Professor Yushchenko developed a programming language which make computers work, describing the computer architecture and its system instructions, methods of computation, and friendly user interfaces for designing and developing databases and knowledge bases for decision support systems, expert systems and methods of learning for them.

She also developed the basic language of artificial intelligence tools for developers of application systems.

Without this, what we use computers and smart devices for would be impossible.

A few days later, I was heading down a farm track to a house surrounded by fields of potatoes. You see, the caller was a farmer as well as having formed this recruitment company. I was pleased it was in County Louth, as I had just moved there, buying a small farmhouse with twelve hectares in the Cooley Mountains. Tullaghomeath to be exact.

The couple who ran the business were every bit the Irish entrepreneur; enthusiastic, knowledgeable and ambitious. Typical of many in Ireland, it is small wonder that the word entrepreneur was coined by an Irishman, Richard Cantillon, from Kerry. He coined this term in his famous *Essay on the Nature of Trade in General* in 1730.

A while ago now!

What became clear was that the problem was process, most especially sequence of actions. They were in the wrong order and visa processing times were extended beyond what Microsoft, IBM and other employers were willing to wait. After a couple of weeks and a few calls to the Department of Justice, I had the process working and the roadblocks removed. *Phew!*

During this time, I reawakened my interest in Ukraine and Ukrainians. You see, it is my curse to be born outside of Ireland, because my family left for work before I was born.

It is a burden I carry today, and it is a regret I will die with. From birth, I was raised in a large Irish family of nine. In our house, there were always extra, and fourteen wasn't too much of a surprise.

Going to the Catholic school, Sacred Heart, was a solid Irish experience for both pupils and teachers alike (the NUNS!), but when I sauntered off to secondary school, there were new names to learn, not Irish ones.

Bohdan Dakyu was one of my best friends. He was Ukrainian and as different to the Irish as the moon from the sun. For a start, he was the only child in his family.

To be honest, I didn't know anything about his Ukrainian heritage until the Convent Garden Party, an annual fundraiser my dad helped organise and built carnival games for. Huge 'roll a penny' wheels, trap a rat, and a multitude of brightly painted games designed to make money. Lots of money.

It was at the garden party where Bohdan danced the hopak… My god, what was that? I asked myself. I had known him about eleven months and hadn't seen him for a while as it was the summer holidays. The music, the costumes and the vibrancy of the dance… I had no idea, being both perplexed and intrigued, as it was far different to our Irish dancing, long before Michael Flatley changed it to the modern exciting versions of today.

I was only coming twelve at the time and I felt bewildered. Bohdan was a quiet, intelligent, fun guy, who every day went to his grandad's house after school and we were friends, despite, maybe because of the fact that I was noisy, adventurous and indifferent to rules, much to the annoyance of everyone but my parents.

Why we bonded, I don't know, but we were both refugees.

My family having left Ireland due to the economic oppression and war imposed by Britain and the ongoing denial of rights in the North, including Bloody Sunday, which occurred on the 30 January 1972, killing fourteen innocent people when I was eleven. This act of barbarity was to escalate into the troubles, as I lived through my teenage years, and lasted till 1998 and the Good Friday Agreement.

Bohdan's family fled the russian KGB, who inherited the NKVD's hatred of Ukrainians; both killed many hundreds of thousands, possibly millions of Ukrainians because of this guttural hatred. It is something that persists today in russia, and which is the fundamental cause of my recent experiences, which I will tell you about later in this book.

Anyway, I lost connection to Bohdan over the years and didn't even think about him until early 1998 when I decided I wanted a nanny for my children. We had three children, a girl who was newly born and two boys, two and seven, who were easy to look after.

Calling my client and giving them work was a pleasant feeling and soon I had my nanny…Svetlana! She would arrive in November, just in time for Christmas.

As I waited outside arrivals in a busy Dublin airport, I wondered what Svetlana would look like, compared to her photograph, which wasn't the best… it wouldn't be long. This was way before immigration control got so very serious and my phone rang.

"Is that Brendan?"

"Yes!"

"This is Sean, I am an immigration guard at the airport. Are you waiting at the airport for someone called Svetlana?"

"Yes."

"OK, she will be out in a few minutes."

"Thanks!"

Svetlana was tall, slender, with boyishly short jet-black hair, and in all leather, very short leather shorts and a jacket, with skin-tight yellow top!

Gulp! Who have I hired?

Turns out, I hired one of the most kind, intelligent and supportive people in life. Someone who would help my children, help me and become a 'sister' to me.

Svetlana is a specialist teacher of visually impaired children working in Kyiv. Awarded for her work after she returned from Ireland, she is highly regarded, but has no interest in the burdens of bureaucracy or management, preferring to hold court in the classroom, where children learn, grow and develop under her gifted tutelage.

Someone I would give money to so that she can buy a house, someone that would provide shelter in that same house when the first attacks happened and someone who I would rely upon in my journey of escape.

Without Svetlana, I would have likely been killed in russian-occupied Irpin, like so many.

That's who I had hired.

Svetlana soon settled in my house and managed the difficult challenge of relationships with my wife and my children. She became one of the family, without any distress or struggle. The children genuinely loved her, and my wife was friendly enough, which was a relief, as she hated the previous girl with a poisonous passion, ultimately leading to her leaving, which was regrettable.

In the early morning, Svetlana would take the children to kindergarten and run back, pushing my little girl, Bronach, in her pram. Collecting them, she would walk them up the mountain, with fun, laughter and some adventure.

A skilled cook, Svetlana soon learned to love Irish food. She also improved her English by sticking yellow post-it notes everywhere... and I mean, everywhere! The house was a picture of post-it graffiti, but I didn't mind.

At the weekends, Svetlana came with us as natural as if she were a member of the family, which she was. It was good to have her company and her friendship, as she was a wise and reliable counsel on any and all matters.

On her first day, we gave her a welcome present, only she dropped it when opening the paper. Svetlana was nervous and tired from travelling. Distraught, I reassured her, we would buy another, and in the morning an exact replica was waiting for her.

You see, in the village of Omeath is a classic Irish shop, 'The Corner Shop' owned by the Mulligans, a fabulous Omeath family.

Its lime green shop sign with red lettering and red canvas canopies, on the corner of the crossroads, in Omeath village has remained the same for seventy years, but at the time I am writing about, it was a mere fifty years old.

Not only is the family ownership the same, created by Paddy Mulligan who built the building and the business, but the treasure trove of Irish giftware, seaside toys, tourist trinkets, plants for hanging baskets and home hardware, such as mops and buckets, plugs and lights make it a must-see destination all of itself, as it retains its stylish charm from when it first opened in 1952.

The shop remains in family ownership and out of the fourteen children Paddy had, Frances, Pauline, Michael and to a lesser extent, Patrick, would be found behind the counter or cleaning the large open area around the shop.

It was from The Corner Shop I had bought the first present, a small white flower vase, decorated with delicate colourful flowers. And it was from there that I bought the replacement, explaining to Pauline Mulligan the events that led me to want an identical vase, causing her to go search the cavernous store and successfully finding a replica.

The first Christmas was a revelation for Svetlana. The decoration rituals, the carols, the children's play, the gifting of so many presents, so much fun and laughter, the decorating of the Christmas tree and food... lots and lots of food, and especially chocolate.

We bought Svetlana a specially made ceramic plate in blue from the local pottery shop, 'Celtic Clays', which now stands in pride of place in her now empty home, just outside of Kyiv, alongside others made by our good neighbour in Omeath. Her kitchen is dedicated to her Irish stay, with the three and a half metre glass splashback, having a panoramic photo of the Cooley mountains and Carlingford screen-printed at the back of the glass. The only one in the world... and it's in Kyiv!

Very quickly, Svetlana became well known in the mountains and the village of Omeath, most especially as 'that girl who runs the roads', since it was unusual then. There was and will only be one Svetlana for my neighbours.

As winter turned to spring and summer, then back into winter, we began to look towards the year 2000. We ignored the warnings that the world will end, that the millennium bug would destroy all computers, and the growing realisation that Svetlana needed to go home as her daughter, Iryna, who was ten, was missing her.

New Year Eve was a special event, with Omeath village and the town on the opposite side of Carlingford Lough,

Warrenpoint, both having massive fireworks displays. The black night sky was lit with constellations of colour, a never-ending cascade that illuminated the sky. Each settlement competing with each other for scale, colour and excitement.

There was a lot of money spent and hangovers to be earned.

Standing together in the warm kitchen looking through the open side door of my house, we stood close, deep in our own personal thoughts watching the changing colours of exploding fireworks and lights in the sky.

Connected but silent, we stared at the sight, both Svetlana and I knew there would be challenges and changes ahead for both of us. Neither knowing what they would be, when they would be and how they would heavily rely on this moment of connection.

For a few months in early summer, Svetlana returned to Ukraine, knowing I had kept my promises. She would return and I would ensure her daughter could visit.

As we adjusted to life without Svetlana, I also struck up the conversation with the Department of Justice. We needed a visa, yes, another one. Yes, for an eleven-year-old. For summer.

Initially, the visa was refused, much to Svetlana's disappointment. I called the department.

The conversation went a little like this.

"So, you refused the visa?"

"Yes, she doesn't have the funds and maybe she will keep her daughter in Ireland illegally."

"Really?"

"Yes!"

Next phone call. "Hi, is this the ambassador?"

"Yes!"

"OK, this is Brendan Murphy and I have a problem."

The kindly ambassador listened and apologised, he really should not have answered the phone.

I would get to know him better later, but it wasn't him or Foreign Affairs I needed. He gave me a name in Department of Justice, who could not have been more helpful.

"Hi, is this Siobhán?"

"Yes!"

"The ambassador gave me your number and I need your help."

Ten days later, the visa was in Svetlana's hands, and all was agreed.

By May, the flowers across the mountains and along the river where I live were in full bloom. Svetlana was back. In August, Iryna came to Ireland for the very first time. She instantly fell in love with my horses and with Ireland, a country she has visited many times, studied and worked here for short periods, and came to shelter from the war, before returning to help refugees, despite the real risks and deprivation.

My home in Ireland is their home in Ireland, for all time.

Our first family visit to Ukraine was transformational.

I have travelled to many countries and climates for holidays and work, including incredible cultures such as Turkey and Oman, but Ukraine made a huge impression.

With three young children and a reluctant wife, we stayed in Svetlana's brother's flat. A large, modern flat with jacuzzi and steam room, which the children loved, especially the jacuzzi with bubbles, although we had to stop that after an incident involving a bubble monster escaping and filling the bathroom. I laughed and enjoyed the screams of the children. Their mother was not impressed, instead, getting angry.

I cleaned the mess and the children slept. No harm done, just fun.

It was hot, hot, hot outside and the city seemed vast. So much walking, metro rides and adventures, but it was hot. Every day, we retuned exhausted, only to be rejuvenated by the jacuzzi.

This was 2001 and Ukraine was nowhere near how it is today. The cars were very unfamiliar, the small busses, *marshrutka*, so alien it was scary, the trams noisily clanked and rattled, their insisted rattle like bell angrily denouncing cars or people in their way.

The children loved eating outside in the hot weather. We went to restaurants designed as villages and ate well. I especially like Shaslik, large pieces of pork or chicken, covered in spiced mayonnaise and cooked on a wood-fired grill, but the salads and breads are very, very tasty.

The children ran in the open fields and went on small paddle boats over shallow lakes that teemed with life, including turtles, frogs and snakes, as well as colourful dragonflies. In the night, cicadas would 'cricket' noisily, a serenade that I was always relaxed by. Sometimes, fireflies would blink in the bushes, but despite patient watching, I rarely found them as they moved about.

Svetlana, her husband Sergey, and their daughter, Iryna, were and are solidly my family, and it was a joy to visit with them.

I still remember the women sitting in the long grass of the park, under trees and by the lakes, singing in the evenings, when the hot sun eased its grip. My children fondly remember the soap baths and bubbles, almost disappearing in an ever-growing soap monster emerging from the jacuzzi.

Sergey was learning to drive at this stage, having

decorated their apartment, which Svetlana bought with her 'Irish money', which she had saved almost religiously.

Being driven in Ukraine was no easy challenge.

Ukrainian drivers are aggressive at best, but Sergey took on the challenge, without lessons, which doubled the stress levels for me as a passenger. Naturally, the children were entirely oblivious and found it fun.

To be honest, being a driver for many years means I struggle to be at peace when driven by someone else. Sergey drove like a man possessed, and not by the spirit of a gifted driver. He earned his nickname, Schumacher, after the racing driver, weaving in and out, hitting the curb and beeping angrily at anyone in his way.

Oh my god, we are all going to die!

Well, we didn't, but it certainly felt like we would.

When time came to return to Ireland, Svetlana stayed behind. Her work in Ireland over, but she agreed to find someone as a replacement. That person was Anna.

While Anna is different, she too is a remarkable person. Again tall, she is quieter and more reflective, but to be sure, she took over the reins and immediately became much loved.

Less of the athlete, Anna was most interested in business opportunities developing her connections with Irish teaching colleges. Anna even met the Minister for Education, making sure she understood everything before she started bringing Ukrainians into Ireland to learn English.

After little over a year, she too returned to Ukraine, as she had two young boys that were growing wild under the easy parenting of her husband and mother.

Years later, these boys are commendable people with solid jobs; one, Igor, having worked for Conor McGregor's 'Fast Fit' business, working on their IT platforms. Something he is highly capable in. Vlad is a highly talented graphic designer and rock musician.

Anna left as the Ukrainian government started looking to open an embassy in Ireland.

I was quick to reach out to the Ukraine government and soon met the first ambassador to Ukraine, Mr Evghen Perelygin.

Our first meeting opened the door to an enduring friendship. Evghen is a calm, poised and circumspect diplomat, in contrast to my 'open all avenues' noisy approach. We did several initiatives, including me setting up the Ukraine–Ireland Business and Trade Association, which I started in 2003, formalised in 2004 and closed in 2007 because the government of Ukraine made things very difficult.

Over this time, I travelled extensively across Ukraine, meeting businesspeople involved in all manner of businesses, from agriculture and food, IT, manufacturing, furniture and retailing. The more Ukrainians I met, the more I realised similarities with Irish businesspeople.

Writing sectoral reports, organising trade visits, holding briefing sessions in the embassy and elsewhere offered an added dimension to my business consultancy. It helped open connections and provided considerable learning experiences.

It has to be said that business trips are truly miraculous. I have lost count of how many competent and capable, married businesspeople left for Ukraine, only to land as unmarried or divorcing millionaires in Kyiv.

Anyway, it was good and taught me more about human nature than I expected. Or wanted!

As the corruption of the Yushchenko and Yanukovych governments bit into every opportunity, and as impending divorce kicked in, I chose to stop my involvement in business and trade, seeking a more stable opportunity by becoming Director of Operations for a group of companies.

While business and trade diminished, my trips to Ukraine, including holidays with the children, continued; travelling in both summer and winter to see Svetlana and Anna, and explore different parts of this large, diverse and endlessly interesting country.

We enjoyed visiting cities, skating and skiing, hot summers and good friends of an ever-expanding circle. It was a comfortable time, with much relief after some fraught time as the marriage ended.

It was in 2007 that I met Sofia, who became a friend, and twelve years later my wife, after two attempts at marriage due to pandemic protocols. Sofia, with her mother, daughter and grandchild, along with a dog and a cat, were my travelling companions across Europe when we sought to escape Putin's military.

But more of that later.

It was 2014, at the time of the brutality of the Revolution of Dignity, between 18 to 23 February, and where 108 civilians were murdered in Kyiv which saw the darkest times, but in a sense, this reactivated my involvement with Ukraine.

The summer before, 2013, I had been in Kyiv and it was transformed into an oppressive state, where even changing money was exceptionally difficult. My experiences of Ukraine and being with friends was far different. Gone was the free and easy life, open smiles and noisy chatting. Now all was very serious and restrained. Oppression is a very serious experience.

Coming at the end of Euromaidan, a street protest which started in November 2013, against Yanukovych's decision to reject a free trade agreement with the EU and seek closer ties with russia, this street protest had been getting darker and darker.

What was, at one time, almost a street festival vibe, with free concerts and street artists, became all out murder. Friends of mine were there, including Svetlana, having supported the previous Orange Revolution in 2004. They were tired of being oppressed and ignored. They were ready to be free. They wanted their lives back; they wanted the right of self-determination.

The barbarity of the forces used against the people was uncompromising, and even today, those involved are not fully known, although some were certainly russian forces, sent by Putin.

Once Yanukovych and the government fled Ukraine to seek refuge in russia, occupation of Crimea started on the same day, 23 February, being completed by 16 March. Immediately following this was the occupation of parts of Donbas, resulting in 1.9 million displaced people.

To my deep dismay and frustration, politicians did not care. In Ireland, in the EU and the US, responses were rehearsed, similar and very definitely absent of any interest. I wrote, emailed... tried to get something done. But no one cared.

Exactly eight years on, on 24 February 2022, Putin would unleash hell on Ukraine, starting with the town where I lived, Irpin, and neighbouring Bucha and Hostomel. Burning their names into history.

Chapter 2
Sofia

It was Aleksandra's idea!

I was visiting Kyiv in 2018, it was after Irish Christmas and as I was alone now, I wanted to enjoy New Year. A sole Christmas after years of children was a somnolent affair and while I managed to push out any feelings of sadness or loneliness, I knew it was something of a façade.

Having worked internationally for months before the break, I had an opportunity for rest, and I hadn't seen everyone in Ukraine since the summer.

I had promised to visit, and a quick response was received. Come for New Year!

It was nice to be in Kyiv, the bright lights, snow and chilly air. Glintwien (aka mulled wine) and Christmas Street fairs, attractions and many, many people. The air was cold and clean, the Christmas tree on Sophieska Square, a monolith of a tree from the Carpathian Forest. So bright with lights and decorations, the tree shone like a beacon.

I planned to stay in Ukraine for a few weeks, having bought my apartment in Irpin in October. My first New Year in my own place in Ukraine. A spacious flat, desperate for repair, but interesting for the stories it would tell from the past and for an unknown future, which included bombing, shelling and automatic gun fire from a tank.

I was happy to stay in my flat. It was quiet and comfortable in an old person's way and my head was full of ideas. The balcony was six metres long, two sets of double doors leading onto it. High ceilings and a big living room. It screamed Parisian flat!

As I sat in the dark, I watched the light, taking up a black marker to mark the outlines. I wanted to change the kitchen to a bedroom and the create a kitchen where the bathroom was. The bathroom would move to the bedroom. Crazy, right?

But as I wandered and traced the outlines, I could see the renovation. I could actually see the end result. The only thing I didn't know was who would do the work. Definitely not me. What little did I know about repairs in Ukraine? Nothing.

I had commissioned a biscuit maker, Oksana Doroshenko from Poltava, who hand painted biscuits to make some presents. Tasty but beautiful. I ordered many, as I wanted each friend to have one. They arrived just on time, by the famed Nova Poshta, early on the 31st. *Phew!*

I had bought other gifts as well. For Sofia, a bottle of Bailey's from Ireland, of course.

I took the *marshrutka* from Irpin to Obolon, these small buses were driven by a few men and I knew them and they recognised me. The Irish guy whose Ukrainian was garbled nonsense. But they accepted my money and stopped when I asked, so that was OK.

Actually, these drivers are Ukrainian heroes, driving all weathers and rarely stopped. Often much put upon by passengers and other drivers, they sometimes had a fit of annoyance and an outburst of anger. Usually when someone didn't pay or wanted a discount. It is one price for Kyiv, fifteen hryvnia or about fifty cent. For twenty-five km.

As we bounced our way through the snow, I was lost in a world of design, the thirty-five-minute drive seemingly completed in a moment.

Walking through the snow on a dark New Year's Eve, I was happy. People on the streets were in a good mood and fireworks glittered and faded, as loud bangs echoed between the large flat complexes.

New Year with Aleksandra and Sofia was very nice. I got some Santa elf slippers and Ukrainian trinkets from Aleksandra, Sofia bought me a jumper. Friends visited and we ate a traditional Ukrainian feast as we watched TV. Daryna was there, her usual impish self, drinking cognac with ease, her laugh growing lighter and louder as the night wore on.

As the friends and Daryna wobbled home through the snow, it came to tidying up. Washing up is my comfort zone, to be honest, and I liked being busy. I am a temperamental socialite, often being quiet, so doing something useful keeps me from drinking till the bottles are empty.

As everything became tidy and clean, somewhere around four a.m., Aleksandra came to me with an impish smile. Sofia was busy with putting the table away and was close.

"Hey, Brendan, why don't you date Sofia? She has no man in her life."

Silence… I simply smiled and said nothing.

I had met Sofia in 2007, a year after my separation.

I was busy working as Director of Operations for a group of companies and with my three children, who stayed with me, one week in two, the change being on a Wednesday.

The marriage was long dead, and the physical separation was a relief. Contact was narrowed to the minimum and the children were settled in the arrangement. I had kept my home, so what was new was mostly with their mother.

We first started by chatting via Skype and it was friendly, light and easy. Not romantic.

In the early summer, I wanted to go to Kyiv, and we agreed to meet. The place was chosen; The 5 Camels, a famous landmark next to the metro station in Obolon, near where Sofia lived. The 5 Camels is a large metal sphere – with 5 Camel statues, suitably painted – which sits atop a shop and pub.

I was half sitting, half lying on a wall underneath the 5 Camels when Sofia arrived.

Wearing a body-hugging T shirt dress that had red and dark blue horizontal stripes, just like Denis the Menace, I thought, Sofia was a true brightness. Straw gold long hair, slim and muscular, suntanned skin. Sofia's smile dazzled the sun.

"Hi," she said, "how are you?"

As I answered, she said, "OK, let's go" and turned to lead the way.

As she briskly walked ahead of me, she had a bounce in her step and assurance in her walk. Not tall, but very energetic.

We had agreed to play badminton and I had brought everything from Ireland. This was going to be fun.

It is a ten-minute walk to Sofia's flat from the 5 Camels and when we got there, we stayed outside. It was a hot day, and the sun was bright in the sky.

We started the game and I immediately realised how competitive Sofia was. This was no game. It was an Olympic contest of wills… winning was crucial. I was in deep trouble.

Although fit and active, I was against an athlete who was both fast and strong. Not tall, Sofia effortlessly met my serves with a response. I did my best to keep up.

Now, I am not bad at badminton and in my teens, I had

played every day with the National Youth Champion who was a friend. I had skills and technique that were good enough to be a decent adversary, but I had little appetite for winning. It simply wasn't what I liked in sport. It is why I like mostly solo sports like walking and mountaineering.

But this was different.

Sofia's delight when she scored a point, her smile and confidence stirred something in me… *Right, I thought. I need to bring my 'A' game.* If I could remember what it was, that is!

During matches with my champion friend, I had defeated her on many occasions. It was never a walk-over and each of us finished feeling that we had worked hard. Now it was time to dig deep and bring my full self to the competition.

As Sofia laughed at another point won, I said, OK, game on. I am Hercules!

The badminton went on for a couple of hours, each one of us not wanting to concede defeat. Neither wanting to accept the loss.

We were still even when a little girl with long dark hair appeared. Her name was Aleksandra, and she was seven years old.

"Hello!" she said, as she walked towards us, having just finished school.

Aleksandra's English was confident, and she had the same open smile as her mother, who it immediately became obvious was Sofia.

Both of us agreed to disagree on who had won and then started to include Aleksandra, whose dislike of losing was greater than the both of us adults. Simply, she was like a wild cat when things didn't go her way. Hissing and spitting with fury.

As our energy and interest waned with the sun, we decided to call it a day. Sofia invited me into her flat, which sat on the ninth floor of the block which stood at the side of the sports area we used for badminton.

As we ascended the lift, I carried much of the badminton equipment, but Aleksandra held her racquet like it was treasure trove. She would not surrender her prize possession, not for any reason.

Sofia's flat was something of a shock.

One room, where they slept, was in good condition but the rest was derelict, and dangerously so.

Of course, a single parent on low wages can't afford to repair an apartment, even if the work wasn't expensive to a well-paid businessman like me, but pride and self-respect meant that Sofia was doing it, all by herself.

What worried me most were the windows, so decrepit that spider webs held the glass in place. Being high above the sports area, more specifically a children's play area with sand, made me afraid.

After some tea, I said my thanks and goodbyes, both of us insisting we had won and agreeing to a re-match. I went off to meet Svetlana and Sergey, who had been working as usual.

A few days later, I met Sofia with Aleksandra and we went ice skating, which is super fun, especially in the summer.

Now skating isn't so popular in Ireland and while a new skating rink had opened in Dundalk and I had taken the children there every Saturday, I was very much the Dad skater... think Dad dancing, only a hundred times worse.

I had no illusions about by inadequacies and accepted the general looks of bemusement of the crowds. The skating rink is on the third floor of a modern shopping centre, and it was packed.

As you may have already guessed, Miss Sofia was a ballet dancer on ice. Fluid, graceful, entirely at ease.

Fortunately for me, Aleksandra was less so and I fell into parent mode. It was a convenient disguise that lasted less than a second.

As the graceful dancer pirouetted and jumped, I shugged along like the walrus on ice I am. Will I ever live it down? NO!

Soup and coffee later, it was time to go. Returning to our usual daily skype calls. Only the condition of her flat bothered me greatly.

Once home, I fretted. The flat was dangerous.

Anna's husband was a builder. I had a large salary and could afford the work. But Sofia would not even think about it, despite my promises that my help had no strings attached. No expectations.

A few months later, Sofia became unwell, due to the poor living conditions, but still she refused. Then Aleksandra needed hospital attention as well. This proved to be the tipping point and it was agreed.

Sofia's apartment would be renovated, in spring 2008.

I spoke with Anna and her husband, making it clear that everything was to be to Sofia's choosing.

I returned to Kyiv for a few days to visit shops with Sofia and explore ideas about the bathroom, kitchen and balcony. Layout, design, colour and fittings. But it was to be what Sofia wanted.

Soon the challenge of repairs began as Sofia and Aleksandra lived with her mother Daryna. Not an easy situation for anyone and with Igor wanting to impose his own ideas, stress points emerged, which I resolved, somewhat bluntly. Whatever Sofia wants, she gets. No arguments!

Renovating a top floor flat with stairs and a lift for access isn't fun, and Igor did his best, helped by Anna. Of course, they were paid, but important to me was that I knew everyone and could understand respective opinions.

Taking down the old balcony was like dismantling a house of cards. Had anything fallen, it would have been catastrophic.

Six weeks later and the renovations were completed, excepting a door that had to be specially ordered. But soon, Sofia's flat was ready for living. Not a day too soon for everyone concerned; as Sofia said, living with your parents isn't easy when you are a mother yourself.

In December 2008, I took Sofia and Aleksandra with my three children, and we spent New Year in the Carpathian Mountains, skiing and enjoying the snow.

It was a very happy time with everyone getting along and having fun. We took sleigh rides into the mountains, went skiing and walked, all six of us. Not quite a family, but not too far off. Platonic friends with few disagreements. We had New Year in the village of Yaremche and it was great good fun.

As years passed, Sofia and I were more or less in touch, but remained as friends. Both of us were busy in life I guess and while I was open to something else, it wasn't practical, with me being in Ireland with my children and Sofia in Kyiv, with her mam, Aleksandra and her friends.

I visited Ukraine many times over the years, but seldom from 2008 to 2014 due to the repressive atmosphere created by Yanukovych and Azarov, along with their pro-russian fellow travellers. Simply, it wasn't relaxed or easy.

After the horrors of 2014, I re-connected more with the country, and started to visit, while Svetlana and Sergey came to Ireland, as did Iryna, on many occasions, having worked for a few summer months in 2010.

To be honest, my connection with Sofia has become a little distant and I was more interested in rekindling business and trade.

I knew that the banking sector wasn't fit for purpose and that business and investors were getting very raw deals.

In 2017 and 2018 I started to develop ideas for a web-based financial platform where businesses and investors could connect. Working with Anna's son Igor, an IT specialist, a small team of my own and Eleks, the large Ukrainian IT company based in Lviv, we built Ukraine Finance Platform, a matching peer-to-peer portal that uses authentication tokens, encryption technology and blockchain which could allow investors and businesses to safely connect and collaborate.

In Summer 2017, I lived in Kyiv for about four months, staying with Svetlana's mother as they redecorated their apartment, but didn't see Sofia at all.

It was September I was with Svetlana and Iryna, sitting in their kitchen.

"Irpin! No, God, you can't move there, Mammy! The traffic is brutal," Iryna said. Ashlynn, her large black Labrador snuffled in agreement.

Svetlana was talking about wanting to move. After sixteen years living in the home, she had bought and decorated using her 'Irish money', it was time for change.

Iryna was twenty-seven and working at Kyiv International Airport, Boryspil, and was living away from home. The flat had done its job and new horizons beckoned.

"Well, it's either there or PetrPavlBorshegovka," said Svetlana.

For me, I had no clue. Never heard of either and didn't care. Anyway, Svetlana said, "OK, tomorrow we will look."

It was late October and a grey day. Sergey drove the little Suzuki to the edge of Kyiv, through narrow roads that were clearly no more than dressed up farm tracks. I could see building in progress all around and it was obvious, Svetlana had a plan.

After thirty mins of travelling, we ventured onto a muddy track which extended beyond the eye could see. Bouncing along and slowly navigating around deep puddles made by construction vehicles, we arrived at a small terrace of two-storey houses, each with land at the front and back.

I was the building expert and I needed to look at them.

We met Sasha, a tall, young man with well-groomed beard, black hair close cut, hands manicured. This man wasn't the builder.

We looked at the houses and I could see problems. The roof wasn't fitting well, some gardens were small. The intention was that the road would service many hundreds of houses and a large international school was being built 250m further down. That meant traffic.

Basically, I didn't like them, and I told a disappointed Svetlana that it was a no.

Having given Sasha my answer, he thought for a few minutes and after some discussion, we agreed to look at some houses that were less well-progressed.

Bouncing around on an even more uneven track, we turned past the school building site and along a lane where single houses were being built.

Not more than 500m from the school was a house that was almost completed and a row of six terrace houses in shell only.

These houses faced the apple orchards which had once fed Kyiv, but were now abandoned, having lost their commercial value.

There was no road at the time, simply a rough piece of ground with a large hole in it, where sewerage, water and utilities were supposed to go. Essentially, we were in a space created by cutting down apple trees.

We looked at all the houses, four of which looked onto the house at the back. The end two facing a large front garden of the house, giving them a more open aspect at the back for sunshine.

Musing about each one, I was drawn to one in particular. Not the end one, as it had roads. I went for a walk in the orchard, just to get a lay of the land.

The apple trees were very old, and apples lay rotting on the ground. Densely planted, the trees were beset with long grass and weeds, walking was difficult, but it was quiet. The air was clean.

Looking through the trees, the second house from the end struck me as interesting and I returned to Sasha, Svetlana and Sergey.

We agreed to talk with the developer.

Heading back to the normal city outskirt roads (with asphalt not dirt), we soon arrived at a small office complex, typical of its style, three-storey, glass-windowed block, outside of which were muddy vehicles typically used by builders worldwide.

We met the developer who went through the masterplan, and we discussed options. I knew what I wanted; it was clear. The large roof space would accommodate a third floor and I wanted that done during the current construction phase (it was bare brick and no floors).

To be fair, the developer was a typical builder. Direct, organised and absent of bla, bla, bla. He agreed, I agreed. We agreed.

Svetlana and Sergey accepted my advice to buy the house and we sealed the deal with a handshake.

The developer would wait a little while but needed a deposit. No problem.

Later, Svetlana and Sergey realised they hadn't the money and the agreement would lapse, forfeiting the deposit. They thought they could sell their apartment and live with Svetlana's mother, but time was against them. Selling the flat was a slow process.

Just prior, my dad had died at the age of 92. He had grown tired of the world and was happy to move on. My share ($1/7^{th}$ of his estate) was a solid lump sum. I decided that it was time to put this money to good purpose and for the very first time, Svetlana and Sergey had a million hryvnia in their bank account.

My money was enough to buy the house and have the additions made. They were delighted, so was I. There is nothing comparable to helping people realise their dreams as far as I am concerned.

In summer, I was in Kyiv for a few weeks and met someone who came from Irpin. They showed me where the *marshrutka* from Obolon to Irpin stopped and a few days later, I decided to go there with my Ukraine finance co-director, who was my ever-enthusiastic assistant, Oleg.

We went to Irpin and walked around, something about the place felt like home and I instinctively knew I wanted to buy a place there. It is a vibrant town of seventy-five thousand with a mix of old and absolutely modern buildings with a large pedestrian central square framed by the town hall and residential buildings with ground floor retail.

This central square is decorated with modern and light monuments dedicated to music and a monument to Taras Shevchenko, Ukraine's national hero and icon. At the weekend, an open market is open adjacent to a large cenotaph commemorating Irpin's dead during World War II.

Irpin was an important front during World War II, when Kyiv was occupied by German forces, and is home to many of the Chernobyl liquidators, the civil and military personnel who were called upon to deal with the consequences of the 1986 Chernobyl nuclear disaster, which is less than forty km away.

We went for a beer before catching the *marshrutka* back to Obolon and struck up conversations with the very friendly people in the bar. It was a hot day, and the beer was cold. All in all, it was good. I liked Irpin!

When I googled Irpin, the name translated from Ukrainian to English in a clear sign. It translated to the word 'Irish'. That sealed the deal.

A few days later, I was back in Irpin and toured the town with a real estate broker. Up and down every street, looking at apartments, houses built under the forest canopy and planned developments adjacent to newly built parks. One street had a small pocket park that was forested. Underneath this cooling canopy of trees were children's play areas and multiple carved wooden characters, taken from fairy tales and popular children's stories.

At the edge of the park was a restaurant and the smell of barbecued meat wafted in the hot air. The restaurant was housed in a modern three-storey building, with banqueting rooms on the second floor and bedrooms on the third, for those preferring to stay overnight. This restaurant was called

Kamelot, ably run by two friends and their wives, all of them were in their early 30s and were in the business every day.

The park was named after the street at the head of which it stood, Pokrovska Street; a tree lined street with old two-storey buildings, the houses built with character after WWII by German prisoners of war.

One apartment on the first floor was for sale, but the agent didn't have selling rights, so he wouldn't let me see it, preferring to show me another, which was on the ground floor on a corner.

This one was dark, and suffered from poorly arranged rooms, largely due to the load-bearing wall, which created a 1m wide corridor that housed a toilet and a bathroom, which made it incredibly narrow. The garden outside was a shared garden heavily overgrown with fruit trees and grapevines, with washing lines running across the garden where washing was hung out to dry.

The buildings lining Pokrovska were built for engineers rebuilding Kyiv after destruction by Stalin. They were very solidly built with interesting features, such as columns, large wooden and metal balconies, and high ceilings in the rooms, especially noticeable in the ones used for receptions and meetings, the others being originally laid out as dormitories and were inevitably small and unusually shaped.

After their original use ended, they were converted into living spaces, the meeting rooms being sectioned to create a large living room and a separate kitchen.

Chapter 3
Irpin, Bucha and Hostomel

My first view of my apartment was a showstopper. On Pokrovska Street, I could see the large for-sale sign on the balcony was still there. It was blue-green, but faded in the sun, having been used many times. In the hot sun of a July day, it looked like it had been there for many years.

Oleg and I stopped on the street, next to a small single-storey brick shop called Alenka, after the famous bar of chocolate, no bigger than a home car garage, and looked at the long balcony with the provocative sign. I wanted to look inside.

We agreed to call at the house and see if it were possible.

When we got to the first floor, we saw an arrangement of four doors of different styles, ages and colours. On the right was a dark brown metal door that was obviously recently installed. It had no number, but by process of deduction we figured out that it was number fourteen.

Ringing the doorbell, which was a black Bakelite button from the 1950s or earlier, we waited a minute. Then tried again. After a few minutes, we heard the noise of a lock turning and the door slowly opened. We were greeted by an elderly lady of medium size and weight, grey-haired and unbowed by age; she emanated a warmth and quiet composure. When she opened the door, the smell of cooking escaped. I was immediately hungry…*Mmmmm.*

Entering the apartment, I could immediately see the layers of changes, modifications, wear and tear. I was enthralled.

There were, in fact, two doors. The modern metal door and some 30cm back, a much older wooden door. Upholstered in black leatherette or vinyl, which was studded with brass studs to make a diamond shape. This door was bent and curved, making it impossible to properly close, so it remained open and entirely useless.

The hall felt large and open, made more so by the 3m high white ceiling with plaster mouldings around the edges. The bare wooden floor painted red, with a large black rubber mat to cover much of it, leaving a red edge of exposed wooden planks. A small mahogany stand with mirror was to the left and there was a huge shelf above, maybe a metre deep, opposite the front door and attached to the far wall, 3.5m distant. Roughly made and painted, it was a monstrosity of necessity, installed by someone when the apartment was full of children and 'stuff'.

Despite the height of the large planks of wood used to make the shelf, painted many times in white, it dominated and made the hall feel smaller than it actually was.

As I looked further, I noticed two large metal mountings set into the wall between the front door and this shelf, to carry a pole that would hold a curtain to keep out the cold in the winter months.

Ahead was an old, white-painted double door whose glass panes had been replaced by wood and painted many coats, roughly, without any preparation or sanding.

To the right was a small hall that led to a bathroom, kitchen and living room. All sparsely furnished. In the corner of this second hall was a wooden shelf with an old phone from the '70s sitting on it.

The bathroom was in poor condition, the rough wooden door was painted white and had a round mirror hanging from a rough unpainted nail. There was no window, so when closed, the door was plain. It was locked by using a hooked metal latch. Simple but effective.

The uneven floor of blood red tiles sloped heavily to one side, the right as you looked in. Maybe 5cm in the angle. The white iron bath had no sides, and the spaces were filled with bowls, basins and clothes for cleaning.

Above the bath were blue plastic tiles, some of which had fallen off the decaying plastered wall, being placed on the lip of the bath for future use… what, I have no idea! Above the tiles, the walls and ceilings were painted white.

Water, heated on demand by a gas boiler in the kitchen, was supplied by a single long tap which swung from left to right, the water shared with a washbasin. In the corner was a toilet that was recently replaced. In front of the toilet, and opposite the bath was the washing machine.

Above the washing machine and toilet was two bare wooden shelves, with glass jars, light fittings and some dubious medicine bottles, each of them heavily covered in greasy dust, that formed a thick film that was unpleasant to touch.

Crowded, to say the least, but interesting, all the same.

The kitchen was a 3.6m square, empty except for a gas heater, gas stove and little else. Brown lino covered the floor and had obviously been down for many decades.

The living room was huge; 6m square and in one corner was an old red sofa bed whose upholstery was tough and sandpapery, covered with blankets, indicating it was here that the owner slept. To the left was a mahogany glass cabinet from the 1950s, absent any keepsakes or mementos, but a few papers, bills and an old modem. A patterned carpet covered sixty per cent of the room but was so dirty that it was difficult to know what colours or patterns were in it.

The cabinet concealed a door which had curved like a banana for reasons unknown; age, dryness, who knows. The door led to a corridor-like bedroom, accessible from the hall. It was also empty except for a wardrobe made from oak. About 2m wide and 5 metres long, it had been used as an oddly shaped bedroom. On the outside wall, a large window and on the inside wall, double doors to the hall.

On the opposite side from the cabinet was a set of double doors with much of the glass replaced with wood and painted over so many times that they would not open easily. This matched a second set of double doors in the kitchen, which did open, to a long 6m balcony that was slightly less than 1m wide.

The balcony had a steel and concrete floor, with parts that flexed, bouncy! It was covered in a thick rubber mat and lined with thin plywood painted a medium colour blue. The windows were single panes tacked in with small picture nails. The roof was a delicate structure of plastic sheets. The whole balcony was fragile, shaking of you opened either of the two double windows.

It was summer and the rooms were cool. Stanislava was nice and explained she wanted to go to live with relatives.

We walked from the apartment up Pokrovska Street and through the forested park. Passing the white wooden arch, guarded by 3m tall wooden soldiers, who were gaily painted in the colours of the soldiers in the universally popular

44

Nutcracker.

The park was full of children and parents playing on or around the play areas underneath the trees, which provided cover from the hot summer sun.

As we walked the circuitous pathways lined with wooden statues of characters drawn from fairy tales and popular children's stories, I was excited.

Passing the curtseying clown that faces the entrance of the park and greets arrivals, we turned right and headed to the three-storey restaurant, 'Kamelot'.

After very tasty shaslik, hot from the wood-fired grill and coffee, we went back to see Stanislava. My mind was made up. I was buying her apartment!

We agreed a price and shook hands.

I saw Stanislava twice more, these times with her son Leonard. First time, he wanted to confirm my intentions and say a little about himself and his mother. He had returned from Moscow for a few weeks to help her sort things out, including clearing debts, gathering the necessary paperwork and bank account.

Leonard was tall and slender. Not quite thin. He was an engineer and was working remotely while in Ukraine. The presence of his laptop and mobile phone was oddly out of place in this old flat, but he had good English and was polite. Very quiet but clearly intelligent.

The second time was the signing over in October. This time, he was a little more self-assured and tried a little post agreement bargaining. I agreed to pay a few hundred dollars for bits and pieces, but it was more a gratuity than anything else. Most probably to pay his travelling expenses.

To be fair, Stanislava had moved by then to Kharkiv and

as he said, they were anxious about the sale. Very worried that it would fall through. I could see no possibility of that.

Stanislava was always in fear that I would pull out of the agreement to buy, especially as I travelled and moving money was problematic. Stanislava had no bank account at the time for receiving money and such a large sum would be seized unless the bank knew what it was for.

I had to travel to Ireland to execute the payment in person, something of a pain as I was working in England at the time.

Having told by my notary, Lavrenty, that everything on their side was OK, I sent the money and five days later flew to Irpin to close the purchase.

Standing outside the notary, which was about 200m from the apartment, on the corner of Poltavska and Natana Rybaka streets, and enjoying the warmth of the sun on an October day, I was waiting for Svetlana to arrive, when I met Stanislava and Leonard. They gave me the keys to a garage I did not know about. A garage of many hidden treasures. It was mine! Cool!

Ownership documents in Ukraine are quite ornate. Blue and yellow, with gold embossing and dense black text detailing the agreement, property and address.

This was a prized document that sat in dust and broken glass until my friend Oleg recovered them on 24 May, three months after the attack started.

Once signed, I had to run to the airport for work in England and it would be a December when I could spend much time. Of course, I didn't leave without five minutes in the apartment, my mind already at peace.

My first weekend in my apartment was in early December and I was very content.

I hadn't changed anything and was sitting in the skeletal remains of someone else's life. It was comfortable and quiet. The community heating system warmed the ancient cast iron radiators silently and I sat on the old sofa-bed soaking up my new home away from home.

That Friday night, I sat with a bottle of red wine in the dark. I watched the lights cast their brightness and marked the wall with a black marker pen I found in the old cabinet.

The wallpaper was once beautiful, ornate, green- and-gold-patterned with birds. Almost Chinese in format, but clearly from somewhere else. In any case, expensive at the time.

Life and living had stamped its mark on all the rooms and as I looked, I started to understand what was original and what was super-imposed by time.

In the morning light, I marked the light of the sun on the walls.

By ten a.m., I had an inspirational idea; a Parisian apartment with double doors, a new bedroom, relocated kitchen, retained mouldings (the ceiling mouldings were 90cm deep) and plaster ceiling roses, but fully modernised to remove dead spaces and darkness.

Being Irish, I hated dark places, doors and small spaces because we have so much grey and dark days. I wanted light. I wanted glass-panelled doors as they were originally made, I wanted a new stylish balcony where you can sit in the shade but enjoy the sun, eat, drink and share stories.

This was to be a new canvas, and I wanted it to be mine, but retaining the narrative of its history, since being built.

I set out on that frosty morning with a mission. Buy a vacuum cleaner and cleaning materials. By noon, I returned with high energy and enthusiasm.

Vacuuming the apartment yielded several heavy bags of dirt. Both the carpet in the hall and the living room were especially heavy with dirt and the weight alone was impressive. Must have been well of 15kg!

Some of the sheets, blankets and other fabrics I took for cleaning, and I was impressed when I saw them returned. Simple dirt comes out well and the vibrancy of the colours were largely restored.

By Sunday, I had cleaned everywhere and put up some Christmas lights in the balcony. Then off to the airport for work.

My Christmas in Ireland was a lonely one.

I had divorced and the children had followed their own paths, primarily following their mother.

I still maintained the traditions and wanted to have a tree with presents as a reminder of the past and as I prospect for the future.

I also had a full Christmas breakfast and dinner. Turkey with everything and a bottle of wine.

I was happy in my Irish home. It was nice, warm and large now as I had built extra to it. The fire is huge and when fully warm, the house is very comfortable.

That year, I decided to buy myself a cuckoo clock! What a surprise when I opened the box, I thought, laughing as I did so.

By 27 December, I was on a plane to my new second home, for New Year. As my contract in England had ended, I was free and I chose to stay for a few months.

After New Year, we were now in 2019 and I invited Sofia to a wooden house with sauna by the river Dnipro.

On the way, I went into Kyiv and bought treats and wine, not realising that I had chosen the wrong place to leave my bag and laptop.

Much to my annoyance, I came from the shop to find the secure locker open, bag missing.

I called Sofia and my friend Gena. I also ranted at the shopping centre, with no success. I suspect that the security people had something to do with this, as the camera was conveniently not working, stopping just before and starting shortly after, the locker was opened.

Losing your possessions, including laptop and passport is a serious pain.

I was determined not to be distracted and insisted to Sofia we would still go to the wooden house that evening as I had the treats and we had booked.

It was a great evening, including dipping into the frozen Dnipro River, using a ladder that had the thick ice removed to create a small square of cold water.

When you are using a sauna, dipping into freezing water when it is -22 degrees is supposed to be healthy, and I enjoyed the experience, although I was worried about losing my grip of the metal ladder and having to swim... Noooo!

I let the frustrations of reporting the theft, getting the crime number and going for a temporary passport pass me by, but I needed to return to Ireland early, to get a new one.

It was six weeks later when I could return again.

In March, I was back in Irpin and met Roman, the husband to the sister of my friend Gena's wife. Roman was a builder and was recommended to create reality from my plans.

I had drawn a detailed map and made marks and measurements on the wall. I thought everything was clear, but

I was not to know that Roman had his own ideas.

His initial response was to send me his own plan, very different from mine, which I rejected several times until, with the help of Gena, he finally and reluctantly agreed my plan.

Having agreed a price, he assembled his demolition team as phase one.

Taking out the wall and removing all the plaster, electrics and pipework was in the plan but nine times Roman was told 'leave the plaster mouldings'. From Monday to Thursday, carnage was visited on the place. On Friday, I left for work, with a plan to return one week later.

The following Saturday, I returned; to be enraged. The mouldings on the wall were gone, only the large ceiling moulding was left, and he had designs on that.

The blistering of Roman was serious and when Gena finished, he was duly repudiated, but still he insisted on being paid for his recklessness.

Given the complications of Gena's marriage to his sister, I reluctantly paid him. All the while deeply annoyed.

While this was happening, I discovered Vadim on Facebook. A master carpenter who posted photos on the door style I was looking for, only my doors would be double doors with small glass panels. Vadim lives in Pryluky, some four hours from Kyiv, but he spent three days a week in the city because this is where his customers live.

Vadim is a quiet, careful man and very well established. He introduced me to Viktor, who would build the kitchen and the slide robes for the hall and bedroom.

As I had fired Roman, I needed a builder and Vadim suggested someone from Irpin to do the work and within a week or so, I had a calmer builder installing the new walls and rebricking walls that should not have been removed. This man was Dima and he started well.

Vadim also recommended the electrician who followed my wiring plan to the last detail, helping me to pick out the fittings so that the quality was to the EU standard.

For a couple of months, everything was going well; Dima also found gas and air conditioning engineers and the work progressed.

For my birthday, we decided to go to Montenegro/Chornogoria for a holiday.

It is hard to describe the beauty of Montenegro, or Chornogoria as it's known in Ukraine. It's incredible. The dry mountains, the ancient cities of Budva and Kotor and the clean bluest blue sea you can imagine.

We landed in Podgorica, a modern city with narrow streets and took the coach to Tivat, where we were staying.

I had booked Airbnb and expected that we would have an apartment for ourselves, but the owner had their own room next to the kitchen and decided to stay, having had some trouble with a friend who she usually stayed with.

Tivat is a modern town with a large Sofia for expensive yachts. Of course, this area has the usual high-end fashion shops, but past that, a large open esplanade opens out to the sea.

Where we were staying was north of the yacht Sofia and after a ten minutes' walk, we were at the sea. Sofia loves to swim and at night would go into the water as I sat on the shingle beach, under the stars and beautiful moon.

It was hot, dry and very nice to wander the modern streets of Tivat in the day, but the bus to Kotor was exceptional.

Our host told us that the bus to Kotor stopped at the bottom of the street and so it did. A usual, ordinary local bus. We were advised to go early, as when the Cruise Ships disembark passengers, the tidal wave of people makes everything very difficult.

We left at eight and watched transfixed as the bus filled the entirety of the narrow road, squeezed between the mountain cliffs and the sea.

Where the road opened our, stone houses faced the road with no pavement. The doors opening right into the road. Opposite the houses, instead of garages for cars, are stone walled inlets for small boats. As we passed these inlets, people sat in the water of the inlets soaking up the early morning sun. *How cool,* I thought.

Arriving to the high walls of Kotor, I recognised somethings from the TV show, Game of Thrones. This was truly a special place.

We were a little early for the market, but some stalls were open. I guess for locals as they were mainly food, especially fish and fruit. We bought some peaches, which were large and very juicy.

We entered the ancient city through a large arched gate in the high stone walls and I was attracted to the crests embedded on the walls. Stone buildings with narrow walls, small pubs and restaurants, we wandered happily, looking at all the shops.

On the other side of the city, we wandered up a river to see a small hydro building then returned.

As we walked back, we spied a sign on a narrow set of stairs, pointing upwards.

We took the hint and walked up the stairs. We climbed, and climbed and climbed, higher and higher. Fabulous views from vantage points until we got to the top. The abandoned ancient city retreat, which served people when the city was attacked.

Simply stunning.

After a while, we returned back to the city for some refreshments and then went shopping for souvenirs.

After five days we decided to move to Budva and stay for the day, before we went home, it being closer to the airport in Podgorica.

Budva is in two parts, a modern gambling and tourism hub and an ancient walled city. We wandered both.

I had promised Sofia that she would experience a lifetime goal of swimming in a Blue Cave and we went to the boats. They were mad money and you needed five or six for it to make sense.

Disappointed, we wandered towards the restaurants where we stopped by a street vendor with black paper and a pair of scissors. He claimed he could make portraits of us and as he joked and laughed, asking us about ourselves, his hands worked feverishly. We were so busy talking to him that we didn't realise that he had cut two exact profiles, one of Sofia and one of me.

Of course, we paid, €10 for both, a bargain I said to Sofia, although she was less than impressed. I took them, after he put them in a plastic bag. They are now on a glass frame in my bedroom in Ireland. One facing the other. Perfect.

As we chatted, I had told this artist that we really wanted to swim in the blue cave but the prices were crazy; €100 each. Once finished, he called to a man drinking a beer on the sand.

His friend was a local fisherman, and he was heading out. For €50, he would take us. "Done deal!" I said.

He asked us to come back in thirty mins, so we headed off for further sightseeing.

His boat was a small motorboat with a hard canopy. Suited for three or four people max; it was comfortable for us.

We headed out and after forty-five minutes passed, the gathering of boats outside a cave.

"Too busy and not interesting," our guide called out over the noise of the engine.

Sofia sat at the front of the boat, and I sat on the canopy, looking at the palatial houses built on the cliffs overlooking the blue sea. I also saw the massive powerboats and billionaire yachts standing out to sea.

Another twenty-five minutes and we slowed. The boat then headed inland towards the cliff. As we approached, a cave entrance emerged and twenty metres away, he anchored the boat. Within seconds, Sofia was in the water and swimming.

I jumped in, but not having swum for a long time was floundering, until our guide jumped in, to ensure I safely returned to the boat and didn't drown.

Sofia had become a seal, swimming effortlessly and without splashing in the blue sea, into the cave and exploring the rocks. Her smile was radiant, and she was extremely happy. This was a golden moment.

After about an hour we headed back, very satisfied. As we returned, I spied a beach, past the fortified old city, and decided that the next day we would explore.

In the evening and the following day, we wandered the ancient city, with its refined shops and music. This was a city for the wealthy. At the back of the city, closest to Tivat, a cobbled path soon led to a stone arch, where a statue of a dancer in the water had been placed. One of the iconic attractions of the city, I took many photos of Sofia here and then we walked further, past a long curved sandy beach, so full of sunbathers that it reminded me of a massive, colourful, seal colony, and on to a rocky outcrop where few people ventured.

Here, the water's edge was stony, but the sea absolutely clean, unlike the busy beach, where the water was oily and littered.

Sofia swam and swam, as I toyed with the idea of jumping off the rocks, like so many others were doing. I was sorely tempted, but after my flawed swimming experiences at the cave, chickened out.

Souvenirs bought aplenty, sea bass eaten, suntanned and much rested, we took the bus to the airport, very contented.

To my pleasant surprise, I returned to Irpin to find that the local authority had replaced the roof with new corrugated cement sheets, with a complete set of galvanised metal gutters and downspouts, making the whole building feel revitalised.

By 2020, they would replace all the old footpaths with new yellow and red paviours, take down the old poplars that were dangerous and plant new trees. They would asphalt the road between the houses, restore the gardens and install new benches.

But the most marvellous thing was the new street lighting, which was LED, emitting a wonderful glow in the dark, that enhanced the atmosphere of the street. When all the renovations were completed in 2021, the whole street looked stylish, comfortable and well-designed.

In the night, the new modern five-storey house on the corner opposite the park augmented the streetscape and its lighting, so that sitting outside or on my balcony was a treat. I loved listening to the woodpeckers drumming in the day and watching the swifts grace the sky, in aerial displays that were majestic. I also loved watching the bats, equally adept at flying, catching insects at night by the light of these streetlights.

Depending on the direction of the breeze, the air would be filled with the perfumes of the forest, or the cool breeze from the two large lakes, on the other side of the park.

By September 2019, Dima's work was finished, and we needed to wait, as thick plaster needed to dry. It would be at least three months, if not longer to wait.

I was working in England from September to December, so my mind was elsewhere.

On 15 November, Sofia and I visited friends in Austria and on the 16th we got engaged over Weiner Schnitzel in the famous Figlmüller restaurant.

A week later, we went to the famous Darnytsya jewellery exhibition, a national showcase for individual and corporate jewellery makers, where Sofia chose a beautiful natural sapphire engagement ring which transitioned from deep blue to oceanic green, a perfect choice as Sofia loves to swim and loves the sea, especially in Montenegro.

I enjoyed Christmas day in Ireland as before and went for New Year to Sofia, my apartment being unfit for living.

I returned to Ireland in February for a week or so, wanting to do some work on a stone wall I was building, separating the lane and the river and to remove some concrete which was left after doing some construction work on my house, extending it to add rooms.

At that time, no one knew what would happen. News since

December of a virus was becoming increasingly frequent and by the end of February, it was in Ireland.

The first week of March was becoming a concern and we were getting married in June. The Irish government suggested a lockdown until May, leaving me little time to prepare.

By the 12th, government and schools had closed down and flights were being cancelled. On the 15th, the Ukraine Embassy messaged me saying that there was a 'last flight to Kyiv' organised by Ryanair. It was flying on 17 March, St Patrick's Day) and I booked a seat.

Desperate, I ran around looking for a special glue for the mouldings in Irpin, calling the Irish manufacturer of Tec7, a tried and well-tested strong glue, exactly what I needed. They told me that it was OK to take onboard a plane. So, I bought 41 kgs, filling a large suitcase to the maximum. I booked extra luggage and went by bus to the airport, taking two cases, the big blue one loaded with glue and a small hand-luggage-sized case with a few clothes. The bare minimum.

Arriving at the airport feeling fearful, I put the large case through, being delighted it went down the conveyor belt.

I then went through the rituals of customs and got to the gate, all the time waiting for my name to be called.

I was extra stressed when waived forward at the departure line. I fully expected a problem. They asked for my Temporary Residents Permit for Ukraine and that's all. Once on the plane, I started to relax.

I was sat on the right-hand side and could see the luggage arrive. I laughed as the loader struggled with my case, but silently cheered as the blue case lumbered up the conveyor belt and into the belly of the plane. *All I need now is to get through customs in Ukraine*, I thought.

The plane was almost empty, with empty rows between rows with one or two people on. The pandemic protocol meant that everything was threadbare.

Arriving at Boryspol, I waited for my bag to emerge, which it dutifully did.

Taking the big bag and dragging it with the hand luggage was no mean feat. In fact, it was painful. As I approached the exit, I was conscious of the officers looking at people and hoped all would be well.

As I approached them, my coat and phones clattered to the floor, and I clumsily went to pick them up, with the blue suitcase crashing heavily to the ground. *That's it,* I thought, *I am screwed.*

As I stood up, I saw that the officers were talking to another person arriving and I squeezed past... then onto immigration.

As they looked carefully at the documents and then me, I was sweating... I was certain I would be pulled up and must have looked suspicious.

Then, to my surprise, the lady smiled and said, "Welcome to Ukraine."

I was in! OooRaa!

With that, I was off to Obolon and Sofia's apartment.

A week later, Ireland issued a 'stay at home order' and restrictions that would impact life for the next two years.

In Kyiv, lockdown also started, meaning I had to isolate for fourteen days, but the restrictions were lifted after six weeks, and a light regime of control introduced. This said, the wedding was definitely delayed to an unknown date.

Despite continuing engaging with potential clients, it was clear that all bets were off and that no work would be available for the foreseeable future.

My answer was to enjoy Irpin, explore and discover my new neighbourhood.

As March headed into May, I decided to buy a car. One that Sofia could use as well.

Looking at cars is always interesting for me, but less so for Sofia. We looked at several cars and tried to buy one, only to be stopped as the seller didn't have the correct paperwork.

Within a couple of weeks, we saw a small blue Skoda 1.2 in very good condition. It was a German import first registered in 2009. It had 79,000 km on the clock and was clean inside and out, although I later realised it had been repainted.

The car ran well, and we took it to a garage for a check. It passed, although needed some small works to the suspension, which, given the Ukrainian roads, wasn't a surprise. Importantly, it passed the 'Sofia Test'. *Phew!* One of the important characteristics of the car was that it was a deep blue. Like the sea off Montenegro.

$4,500 later, all documents were checked, and it was mine... I mean ours; ownership was documented in Sofia's name for convenience! Despite the lockdown, we had managed to buy our car, now called 'Baby Car'.

Baby Car was my freedom to roam and Sofia's opportunity to drive. It was a very wise investment. How wise? Baby Car saved our lives.

Within another week, Sofia started to learn to drive with me. Driving in Ukraine is challenging as many drive aggressively, enjoying beeping in a split milli-second when the lights go green, driving on the inside lane and cutting across other drivers. As for speed... well! Fast, very fast.

Teaching Sofia was a difficult experience for both of us,

and I suppose my concerns for life and limb got the better of me sometimes. To be fair, Sofia is a good driver and very cautious, but this opened the door for recklessness by other drivers, creating countless near misses, not all of which I could ignore.

Sofia also took lessons and the driving test, passing on the second attempt.

Almost immediately, though, I wanted to explore, sometimes with Sofia, other times on my own. Driving to Irpin from Sofia's flat became so easy, but going to the forest, lakes and small villages near Irpin was now possible.

While Sofia liked picnics, she isn't an open traveller. She wants a destination, while I am happy to wander.

Of course, Baby Car wasn't needed for local exploring. My apartment is 50m from the forested Pokrovska Park, five minutes from the lakes and ten from the forest and Irpin River.

My first visits to Irpin lake were in winter when thick ice covered the water. Fishermen would make holes where they would try to catch fish and on Epiphany, which is January, people cut a cross in the ice and, having blessed by a priest, enter the freezing water, going underneath at least three times. *Brrr.*

But the lake in May was very different. It was hot, the sun shone and much to my surprise, many turtles sat on floating logs, silently warming together.

When I first saw them, I pushed through the tall lakeside grasses to see them better, only to emerge from this to see a large turtle walking on the path I had just left.

It is often said that turtles are slow. Not this one!

The turtle ran along the narrow path and into the sandy forested area, where lizards and snakes can be found.

In the young pine trees, many birds will dart and secretively hunt insects, of which there are many, giving reason for the very large spiders who love to cast their webs across the path, causing some discomfort and occasional alarm, especially for those in swimwear, walking to the sandy beach next to the lake waters.

At the beach there is a bar, small restaurant and places where you can book wooden huts with tables.

These tables, with their front roofs look suitably tropical and with a strong sun, it isn't hard to imagine, except for the songs of the frogs, the birds and the skyline of buildings on one side.

Beyond this lake lies another, much more natural lake, where fishermen silently fish and where walkers navigate the narrow paths, to the sounds of singing frogs and the *plop, plop, plop!* sounds they make when they launch into the water away from the sounds of footprints.

This larger lake is edged by the railway line and the road. Being very large and less popular for picnickers, it is largely a nature walk, except for a field near the road, where outside weddings are held at the weekends.

These lakes have enormous interests for the nature lover and many hours can be spent walking the 6km walk around them.

On the other side of Irpin, through a wall of new high-rise developments, the many forests and lakes beckon. With Baby Car, we could explore villages like Zabucha, Vorzel and Dmitriivka, as well as places further away, such as Vyshorod, Kyiv More (Sea of Kyiv, a large reservoir), Pidnovo, Chernigiv, Odesa, Chernivtsi, Khmelnitsky, Kam'yanetsk podil's'kyi and the small skiing resort of Migove.

It also meant that we could go to Irpin's conjoined sister, the town of Bucha, which is on the other side of the River Irpin, and which can be accessed through a number of roads, most popularly via Soborna Street at the junction marked by the Giraffe Shopping Mall, which would be the scene of intense tank battles in March 2022, resulting in photos that went viral across the world.

Before we get to Bucha, I will describe the small settlements around the two towns. Simply, they nestle in extensive pine forests, with hidden lakes and large open areas, which stretch beyond the eye can see.

Hugely popular for walking, cycling, picnicking and swimming, people have very many options to explore.

While of course there are creatures of bad habits who dump their waste, there are others who every year go out to clean. In June of 2021, I did this with my neighbours, collecting a very large skip of trash left at the banks of the lake, but in June 2020, I went by myself, finding a beautiful spot in the forest to spend the afternoon, while Sofia worked, and collecting the trash till it was spotless, after which I rested, with some tasty treats I had bought. The five bags I filled were dropped off at the municipal waste collection centre; job done!

In these areas, there are village restaurants with small museums, ideal for extended stays, especially long weekends. These are small collections of wooden houses or cabins with a central restaurant offering breakfast and evening meals.

They are typically styled a 'Ukrainian Village' and really nice. Not only are you in a quiet area surrounded by nature, but there are many small quirks to interest you. In one, there is a large dog kennel, some 5m up a broken tree in the forest. I have photos of me inside this kennel, it is a great place to hide.

Almost everywhere, there are artefacts of Ukrainian traditional life from years ago.

Nature is in abundance in these areas, with the sounds of woodpeckers drilling, squirrels scampering and signs of both badgers, foxes, deer, pigs, rabbits and elk, who roam silently and can occasionally be seen early in the morning crossing roads.

I remember being told about this by a friend, and by coincidence someone shared a photo of one they drove past as they returned to Kyiv at five a.m.

The food is often salads with meat or fish cooked on a wood grill. Very tasty. Of course, soups are offered, especially borscht. Pizza, burgers and other international foods are popular, as is Varenyki, cakes and sweet pastries, with tea or coffee.

Bucha, as I have said, is Irpin's conjoined sister and the separation is the River Bucha, almost invisible really.

What was once a small settlement has been developed into a city of modern high rise apartment blocks, parks, green spaces, restaurants and local shopping areas.

Urban living in a natural environment, I suppose; many people who live in Bucha are professionals from Kyiv, young families, mostly recent arrivals. Outside the built-up areas, modern single houses hide from the summer sun in the forests, many being architecturally individual and modern.

I have friends who live in such houses and enjoy sitting in their gardens and the trees creak and groan in the wind. Throughout the year, the air smells of forest, especially in the summer, when the smell of pine trees wafts across both Bucha and Irpin.

Hardly any of these buildings are more than fifteen years

old.

On the road to Kyiv, Bucha ends and gives way to Hostomel (pronounced Gostomel), a much older village, with a simple string of houses and some factories... oh, and of course Antonov Airport, the private airport of Antonov, whose Myria plane would occasionally fly over my home, returning from international missions transporting aid and material for the UN, national disaster relief organisations and private organisations such as Boeing.

Yes, Myria is the world's largest plane, so big that it can accommodate another plane. Well, it could until the russians destroyed it and Hostomel Airport on 24 February 2022.

But life wasn't all relaxation and while I was pitching international businesses for work, with no success, progress on my apartment was needed.

In the summer of 2020, my mind turned to two practical challenges; one being the balcony, the second being the replacement of the mouldings.

Finding a company that could do the moulding work was extremely difficult. The design was very large and complex pattern. I didn't want a token modern coving, I wanted something authentic.

Svetlana found a website for a company in Ternopil and suggested I take a look. I found two pieces that together would work; one very large to go between the ceiling and the wall, the second, which would underpin the first and stop it falling, was straight. Together, all 30cm of them resembled what had been destroyed by Roman.

I ordered the mouldings, all sixty-four metres of it and waited.

By the end of June, the mouldings were delivered. What

a disaster!

The delivery driver arrived, and I was very pleased to see the large wooden crates loaded off the truck; one for the big moulding, one for the straight.

On opening the wooden boxes, I saw the mouldings bound in bundles; two large ones together and four straight ones together.

The company had supplied them wet, which meant they were like a biscuit after dipping in tea. While they were OK in their packaging, bringing them upstairs to my apartment was too much; they simply broke.

There was only me and Sergey to do the work and we did our best to minimise the breakages. God love the delivery driver who waited patiently as we exhausted ourselves running up and down the stairs. Because they were wet, they were very, very, heavy.

Once we got all of them in, we assessed the damage. Seven pieces of the straight were broken and two of the large.

I signed the document and paid the driver.

While I was mystified as to why they would send the mouldings wet and fragile, the owner of the company was ballistic.

The manager had a tough time and apologies flowed. It would take a few weeks to make the replacements, as the press had to be changed for each design and other orders were being made. That said, a month later and I had the delivery.

There was a problem though. They were wet and couldn't be handled. I had to carefully lay them to dry. Something that would take three months in the warmth of summer. That meant I had to wait till October, otherwise they could break whilst being put in.

By whom and how I could get this done was a serious question, especially as they were so very heavy. I hoped they would lose weight as they dried!

Our wedding in July was postponed by the wedding service due to Covid and while I was supposed to renew my residency permit, the office didn't work, so we were looking at September.

As compensation, Sofia and I went on holiday with Svetlana and Sergey, driving down to Hrybivka in our separate cars.

We drove down to Odesa from Kyiv a couple of days before Svetlana and Sergey, wanting to visit Odesa, the famous port city which predates its fictionalised russian history.

The first settlements were built by Zaporizhzhya Cossacks who had fought the Ottoman Empire and pushed them from Ukraine. There is a famous painting showing these men around a table, laughing at demands to surrender. Their response was to invite the Turks to do the same, following up the invitation with attacks that put the enemy to flight.

Having attacked and successfully taken the important Khadzhibey fortress, Catherine the Great had them ethnically cleansed to the Kuban region of russia in 1792. Something that Putin has repeated in 2022.

I had read about the "Sotnikovska Sich" cemetery just outside of Odesa on the Hadzhibey Road and wanted to visit it. Sofia had disdain for my interest in all things 'antique' and didn't want to go.

Sofia will often pass a remark on my love of antiques, to which I reply, "It's why I love you!"

Fortunately, she likes to sleep long in the morning and since we had driven through the night (to avoid heavy traffic and hot sun during the day), I took my chance and drove the fifteen minutes from the hotel to the cemetery.

Having driven through the port complexes on a narrow unsigned road, using Google Maps, I progressed to what became a lonely narrow road, whose concrete base was in sections, so would cause a bumping sound as I drove over the cracks… *bump, bump, bump, bump.*

On the right, industry gave way to salt marshes, with an occasional building; on the left was a bluff or rise, that was formed of Limestone, green with trees and vegetation. They call this slope Shkodova Gora (Shkodova Mountain).

It was a hot morning, despite it being early, and I couldn't find any evidence of a cemetery.

I stopped at a small shop, where a *Marshrutka* had dropped people off to check the map and noticed they were a group of tourists who headed off clearly with some purpose in mind.

I went into the shop to ask directions and the man pointed to where I had driven. 500m, that's all.

I drove back and stopped at a house. Ancient-looking but updated. Obviously, a family lived there.

Initially, I was doubtful but as I looked, I noticed an overgrown car park at the side of the house and parked there.

Getting out of the car, I saw a narrow path going up the hill and decided to follow it.

The house had a high garden wall, and I was very doubtful about this and nervous about trespassing, but once I was past the high wall, a smaller wall traced up the hillside. As I approached this low wall, I saw a small gate, familiar to me as a typical cemetery gate and there it was. Wow!

The cemetery was unkempt and difficult to find paths. But

there, clearly, were limestone crosses of grey limestone and near the top, almost central, I could see the famous cushion gravestone.

It was very hot. The heat came from the ground as well as the sun. Dried grasses and weeds stood to knee-high, many scratching my bare legs. As I wandered and took many photos, lizards, insects and God knows what skittered about.

An incredible place, I stayed there an hour, conscious that it felt like someone's back yard, me being clearly visible from the back windows, but this small cemetery was special.

The Cossacks created the cemetery in 1775 and named after the family of the Cossack Sotnichenko. The earliest dated stone is 1791, but there are many unmarked stones and obvious graves with no stone.

These Cossacks earned money in the Kuyalnik Liman salt mine and in local quarries. In time, they became residents of Hadzhibey after the Ottoman left, and subsequently became the first inhabitants of Odesa.

But prior to that, they created homes by cutting holes into the limestone of Shkodova Gora and lived a Troglodytic existence. These homes you can find abandoned if you walk around the area, which is what I did after visiting the cemetery.

When I returned from exploring the narrow windy tracks, with their old houses' olive and fruit trees and farm animals, I met a man who lived in the house. He was tinkering with his car and oblivious to my presence. I guess I was being oversensitive.

On getting back to the hotel, Sofia had just woken (it was after 11.30!) and we explored Odesa.

I have to confess that at first sight, Odesa didn't impress me. I think it is because so many people talk expansively about the city and created an impression that reality couldn't match.

The famous Potemkin stairs are just stairs, leading down to the port, which is a mix of old and modern buildings.

The streets are OK architecturally, although in parts many need serious repairs. The main tourist area, which includes the Opera House, seemed just OK, but when we returned again in September, it was more attractive, on second sight.

The beach there is through a very large park and walking in the hot sun was tiring, but necessary, as Sofia would say. The famous beach itself has a large area of concrete in one part and it is this that features in the many films that created Odesa's romantic reputation.

In any case, it was interesting to spend a day and a half there, but soon it was time to head towards Hrybivka to meet Svetlana and Sergey.

Hrybivka is a small strip of family-owned hotels, shops and restaurants next to extensive golden sandy beaches and the warm blue waters of the Black Sea, about an hour or so west of Odesa.

Typical of seaside places everywhere, the beach was equipped with banana boats, peddle boats, plastic couches and umbrellas, but we preferred to use our towels under a green umbrella which I bought at the small market, halfway down the row of shops, selling T-shirts, tourist merchandise, spare batteries, chargers and food.

We stayed at a small hotel used by Svetlana's work colleague. All the rooms on the second floor to the fifth had balconies and our room overlooked the 'strip'. A narrow road lined with small kiosks, shops, restaurants and hotel. Where we were was next to a much larger hotel, the courtyard of which led to the sea. Five minutes' walk, if you are slow.

Behind the hotel were large three-storey wooden houses where families could live in self-contained flats and there were gardens for sports and a second one for barbecues. Toilets and washing facilities were built in the gardens, which had been planted with many brightly flowered shrubs.

The atmosphere was relaxed and family oriented. Quiet, despite the number of guests, most especially the children.

Such holidays are unusual for me. I prefer activity, but sitting in the sand, swimming in the warm blue waters, exploring the shops, was a nice alternative, for the first few days.

Sofia loves the sea and swimming. She would swim far and remain in the water for very long. I was content to soak up the sun or sit under the green umbrella I had bought (Yup, typical Irish person!).

Wandering the shops, market and restaurants provided relief from the hot sun, whilst locally produced wine on the balcony at night gave us peace.

Ukrainian people are typically quiet and by 10.30 the darkness of the night had set in. It was full moon while we were there and it sat above the sea, which was visible from where we sat.

We were doing fun things. Sofia had that 'feet in a tank of fish' experience and laughed uncontrollably, till she couldn't stand the sensation. We had breakfast in different places, often salad, blinchiki (pancake) and coffee, while later we would eat a light dinner.

Neither of us eat much, nor drink heavily, but Sofia loves fish, so it was sea bass, sea bass, sea bass for her. Every day, she would save some and take it for her lunch by the sea, along with a large bag of Semichki, salted sunflower seeds, that see would compulsively eat at the beach, like a demented mouse. Taking the mountain of black seed cases to the bin when she grew tired of the beach.

By the end of day two, I was bored. I really am not a beach person.

The Odesa region of the Black Sea is important to Irish history, in that it is this area that our people came during the great migrations after the ice age and I wanted to explore. There were three places I wanted to go, but before I got my chance, Svetlana suggested we go to Akkerman Fortress (its Turkish name), also known as Bilhorod-Dnister fortress (Ukrainian name) in Bilhorod which sits on the western bank of the Dniester Estuary, close to the Moldovan border, most particularly Transdniestria, which has become a russian-occupied territory notorious for smuggling and trafficking.

Sergey drove to Bilhorod as Sofia and I sat in the back of his Suzuki. The warm air meant that open windows were required.

We passed through the holiday town on Zatoka, with all its rides, attractions and market and up past Roksolany and Shabo.

Famous for wine, cognac, olive oil and oranges, we passed fields and fields of vines, olive trees and orange groves. Their disciplined lines stretching across fields.

In Shabo, there is a modern visitor centre, but other family chateau also allow visitors. Small stalls offer fruit, wines and fish.

Bilhorod is an ancient city with considerable industrial areas. The small streets with cobbled roads are only part of the city but we went through them to get to Akkerman, a large fortification built on the remains of the Greek City 'Tyras' which remained until fourth century, having been attacked by Goths and Huns.

Over time, the city was in the hands of Kievan Rus, the Kingdom of Hungary and the Principality of Galicia Volhynia until it was taken over by the Mongol 'Golden Horde'.

It was a trading city of the Genoese, who, after the Mongols took over, got agreement that the Genoese could still manage it. The Lithuanians took over the area in fourteenth century, losing the area to the Principality of Moldavia.

Anyway, the fortress is a massive walled city whose walls and armoury buildings remain intact, although little is left of the city houses and commercial buildings.

As we walked around the vast open area that once was a thriving residential and commercial settlement, which was home to twenty thousand Moldavians, Greeks, Genoese, Armenians, Jews and Tatars, I got a call from my great friend Carol O'Connor and soon was separated from Sofia, Sergey and Svetlana.

Taking the opportunity to explore, I looked over the walls across the estuary, called Liman, and saw Roksolany, a small village that hid the lost Greek city of Nikonion and the Dniester Canyons. A place I would explore the following day.

After an hour and a half exploring, I found Sofia, Sergey and Svetlana sitting in the shade under a massive tree and with some indignation (we thought you had disappeared!), we went to have pizza at a local restaurant and returned to Hribivka.

When we returned from Akkerman, we walked the narrow street in the dark evening and bought some locally made wine… Sofia and I sat on our balcony drinking the first bottle as a giant moon rose into the darkness. In the morning, I planned to watch the dawn, then venture to Roksolany, on my own, since Sofia had her designs on sleep, the sun and swimming.

Dawn was a funny affair. Early, it was dark, and no one was about. As the sun rose, yellows and blues and greys lit the night sky till the bright ball of the sun rose from the sea, with only me and a couple some 200m away to witness it.

After a shower and breakfast, I headed off in Baby Car, first to Zatoka, then right to Roksolany.

Passing the village, I took a left onto a farm track. Clouds of dust billowed behind me as I headed towards Lake Liman, the name if the estuary.

In reality, the dirt track was between crops and there was no one to be seen, not even a farmer. After about ten minutes, I came to a T-junction with a second dirt track.

This one even less well-travelled, but this one lined with trees on one side. As I bounced down the track, I saw a gap in the bushes and drove into some uncultivated land and stopped. Here it was, the Dniester canyons, unheralded, unsigned and absent any people.

Walking on the tops of these deep ravines, I could see that the soft sandy soil easily collapsed, but the wildflowers, insects and views across Liman were distracting. That was until I realised, I had walked across an emerging break in the soil surface and stood on a large lump of ground getting ready to fall into the water 200m below me.

What a wakeup call!

I decided to return Baby Car to the track, on the grounds that no explanation would satisfy Sofia, who had just started to learn to drive.

Some 200m along the track, I noticed a stone block with ancient writing. I stopped the car and walked the thirty metres towards it.

Nikonion.

Other than small hills and dips in the surface, few indications of an ancient city could be seen at first, but as I wandered and explored, I noticed digging. In these places, human bones, shards of clay and pieces of broken tile could be found, exposed and on the surface, dug up by treasure seekers, illegally looking for coins and valuable artefacts from ancient Greece, as the city is reputed to have made coins, including some with the name of the Scythian King Scyles on, who may have his tomb there, but as yet is unfound.

As I walked, I saw the cut in the sand leading down to Liman. I decided to drive down this long track, obviously made when the city was thriving, many hundreds, in fact, over two thousand years ago.

My imagination was running wild. Thinking of what life would have been like. As I got down to the water's edge, I could see signs of earthworks, foundations of landing places and buildings. It appears that part of the city had fallen into the sea, much like Atlantis.

Founded in the latter part of 600BC, the city was attacked by the Macedonians associated with Alexander the Great and abandoned after it was destroyed by the Goths, at the time of the great Migration when people from this area migrated across Europe, some of whom arrived in Ireland. So, my antecedents! So cool!

On my way back, I passed the many olive trees and vineyards, stopping at a deep green grove of trees, to fins that they were orange trees, in full fruit, but not quite ready.

I have never seen orange trees in the 'wild' before and it made for an interesting conversation.

Well, not for Sofia!

That evening was a replay of the one previous, but I managed to persuade Sofia to come with me and look for flamingos. As an animal lover, she couldn't resist.

We drove past Roksolany and north on the eastern bank of Liman. I had thought that we would see flamingos at the top of Liman and was disappointed to find that tall marsh grass obscured everything.

This area was full of boats and small craft on the River Dniester, the sides of the river full of cars. Up ahead was the border of Moldova, so after a short while I turned round.

Before we got to Roksolany, I turned right and down a very steep single-track lane. Getting to the bottom inch by inch. Large holes and landslides made huge holes in the road and Sofia was far from impressed. That said, Baby Car did her job, no bother!

At the bottom, people were picnicking by the waters of Liman and narrow wooden boats, similar to the Irish Currach were drawn up on land, lain upside down. One of these long, thin, back boats served as Sofia's seat as she gazed over the water and ate some food we had brought with us.

To improve Sofia's mood, I suggested she swim, but she pointed to a man 600m in the water, wading knee-deep through the shallow water, which is attractive for flamingos, but not that day.

To make peace, I offered that she drive back and she agreed, as long as I drove back up the narrow lane.

Sofia is a good driver, but nervous, which causes danger. I am a driver but no instructor. I struggle not to be afraid when she gets nervous, but on this day, with the sun shining and warm air all around us, she drove 20km without hassle, then drove back again, to experience three runs without any incident. 60km... no accident, *phew!*

After a week, we headed to Kyiv, sunburned, rested and ready for wedding preparations.

Chapter 4
The Wedding

We returned to Kyiv from Hribivka by a slightly different road, missing out much of Odesa. As we drove the first 50km, we stopped to buy fruit, most especially a watermelon, which Sofia adores and lives off for much of the season.

Returning with bottles of locally made red and white wine, cognac and souvenirs, we drove to the main Odesa–Kyiv Road, reaching the road bridge in good time, only to wait forty-five minutes as there were roadworks.

The bridge is a two-lane highway being made slightly wider. It crosses an inlet of the Khadzhibey Estuary and in the summer sun, we baked.

Once past the road works, we headed north to Kyiv, some six hours away.

The holiday soon passed us by, and Sofia told me that the wedding service had started to work. Great! Let's agree a date.

As it was 8 August, we decided that the 12 of September would be the day… and so it was. Well, kind of. Part 1 really, but we didn't know that yet.

The wedding service for Ukrainians marrying foreigners is provided by the Central Palace of Special Events, a unique tri-cornered building on Peremohy Avenue in Kyiv.

When we went to book in May, we had been shown the green room and the blue room, almost identical, and despite

Sofia's love of blue, we chose the green room. It's light, air space, filled with sun, its wooden lacquered floor offering an openness, with large ornate gold chairs with green plush seat and insert at the back to give comfort to our guests. It could hold two hundred easily but our intention was for one hundred and fifty or so.

Once the room, wedding officiant and photographer had been re-booked, documents submitted and checked, we were already to prepare the invites. Finally!

It took us a couple of days to prepare the list, which we did separately. Then we emailed them off.

A week later, Sofia suggested we watch one of her favourite films, Мой ласковый и нежный зверь (My Sweet and Gentle Beast) based on a story written by Anton Chekov.

The film was from 1978 and was a costume romance and set in late nineteenth century manor and estate in the forests of central Russia.

The forester's daughter, Olga Skvortsova, is a beautiful girl of nineteen. At first glance, Olga is natural and easy ("an angel in the flesh"), but later it turns out that she is worldly, prudent and vain, according to the description. For me, I had no clue what was going on.

Three middle-aged men who live in the estate and its surroundings fall in love with her, of course, these being a fifty-year-old gloomy widower Urbenin; even older, but youthful and playful, Count Karneev and a stately handsome man, forty-year-old judicial investigator Kamyshev.

So, it was a romance, melodrama, murder mystery and I wasn't sure if it would end well.

It didn't; she dies, stabbed by her own knife, murdered during a picnic by someone unknown, till the surprise ending, which came as a blessed mercy...for me.

Anyway, there's a big wedding scene in the film which includes a waltz. It is a hugely popular scene and replayed in many places. It was unknown to me, but Sofia's most fervent wish to dance this waltz at her wedding.

Wait, what!

I could see that Sofia was nervous about my reply and I wanted so much for her to be happy, so I simply said... OK, no problem.

Inside I was having that argument Gollum had with himself (Sméagol) in Lord of the Rings, The Two Towers. *Dance! Don't Dance! Dance, I say! No, it will be a disaster, I say! Dance...* Hmmm, OK!

A few days later, Sofia suggested dance lessons. *Oh god!* I thought. *This is going to be difficult.*

And then I got a FB messenger message... when Sofia was sitting not more than two metres away.

It was a YouTube link, to Mark Terenzi, singing his song 'Love to Be Loved by You'.

I hesitatingly clicked the link and nervously waited for it to start.

The guitar started first then...

'I can't believe I am standing here,
been waiting for so many years, and today,
I found the queen to reign my heart...'

Acutely aware I was being watched, I smiled. I genuinely liked it as the words spoke to my own feelings. This was good.

In fact, it was great!

Listening to the full 3m59s, I was happy, knowing that

fearful eyes were on me. What I said next mattered. Mattered very much.

I managed to squeak… "That's perfect."

So, all decided.

Not quite!

A week later, Sofia said. "We have to meet Dima."

"The builder?" I asked.

"No, the dance teacher. I sent him the video and the song, and he agreed to teach us."

"Teach? Me? Wait, you don't understand, I am Irish… have you seen how we dance? I…*aaaaahhh*, OK. When?"

Two days later in the evening, we walked to Art Bratyslava, an art and dance academy ten minutes' walk from Sofia's apartment in Obolon, to meet Dima.

I was surprised how composed I was when waiting. There were many people in the dance hall, and we had fifteen minutes to wait, until Dima was free.

Because I didn't know him, I had no clue until this young slender and lithe man approached with a sympathetic smile. Dark-haired, he had the body of one of those salsa dancer types. I have the Irish sack of potatoes body… slender version, I know, but definitely soft-centred. This man was an athlete!

"So, you want to dance, ha?" he asked, very serious, but with a sympathetic expression on his face.

"Errrr yes, but, but but—"

"No buts," and soon, we started with the simple steps. And I mean, simple.

Sofia was anxious and wanted the steps to be exact. I wanted to survive the ordeal.

Thankfully, some missteps by Sofia meant Dima could assert his authority on the pair of us, made unarguable as he took me for a spin and my steps were good.

So, we started and after an hour and a half we had learned the opening of the dance, which was going to be epic!

It would take four lessons to get the whole sequence practiced and we also tried at home, including the morning of the wedding. The video shows we nailed it, including the fall and catch, eight-step square, crossovers, waltz and the high lift at the end, around the square made by the tables.

Ten points for me and Sofia, I thought. Everyone cheered and Sofia was very happy.

I needed a drink! I had abstained till that point.

But, before we got to the dance, there were other things to do.

During this time, I was busy with the balcony and developing proposals for potential work. I am an International Business Consultant and would engage with senior business leaders and their teams, but as time advanced, I needed to go to Fortetsa to finalise the food and refreshments.

Sofia couldn't go so I went with her friend and work colleague Iryna and Sofia's daughter, Aleksandra.

Iryna had run a corporate hospitality business and Aleksandra was a trainee chef. I know, I know, what could possibly go wrong?

When the restaurant manager came to meet us with the menu list, everything started sedately enough, each one asking questions about recipes etc. But as time went on, it descended into a competition of who could order what and the ever-growing list of what we want became substantial.

As I listened to Iryna and Aleksandra compete, I could see the manager's eyes getting bigger and bigger. I decided to say nothing until the end, when I asked that the menu of 'provisionally ordered' food would be emailed to me so I could discuss it with Sofia and finalise it.

Once arrived, I laughed. 1.2kg of food each, plus bread, cake and alcohol. That was a lot.

Sofia and I pruned the menu down and we were happy to agree. Of course, both Iryna and Aleksandra were offended and said everybody would starve, but at the end of the evening they filled three very large containers of uneaten food proving, to me at least, that Sofia and I was right.

Buying the alcohol was my job, but the wine, Champagne and cognac were of Sofia's choice. For each table of six, there was 11 bottle Vodka, one 750cl bottle Cognac, three bottles of red wine and three of white. The Champagne toast was enough for three glasses each.

When an Irish man marries a Ukrainian, you need drink.

Sofia ordered the cake and the Korovai, an ornate wedding bread of different dough colours, with many birds, flowers and other designs. We bought the brightly coloured wedding towel in the market, where stalls of traditional clothes and wedding supplies, suits and dresses are sold.

Sofia chose a shop near Shevchenko University to look for her wedding dress, despite a world-renowned Ukrainian village, Voloka, being dedicated to making dresses, selling them for export as well as the massive 35-hectare Kalynivsky Bazaar in Chernivtsi. I drove her there. She had decided that she needed no fuss and no arguments when choosing her dress, so Aleksandra, Iryna and her other friends were out.

I had supported Sofia when she went for her wedding dress by saying little other than admiring words.

The shop, Inessa, on Lva Tolstoho St, 17, was expensive, offering beautiful dresses from Italy and the US. They had a store in Odesa and in Kyiv, and when we were there, it was busy with future brides and their mothers. I was the only man but didn't worry myself over it.

The shop had a busy calm, efficiency, the assistants attentive and professional, without any hyper sales techniques; they knew the dresses sold themselves.

One woman in her 30s was choosing a dress and when she came out from the dressing room to show her mother, looked stunning, except for her tattoos, which consisted of a full sleeve and back. The dark depictions on her skin would look cool in any other circumstance, but in the wedding dress they just didn't work. The future bride was crestfallen.

To my surprise, the assistant would offer her a white skin-tight top that covered her skin and when she returned, it worked, and she seemed happy. Well, they went off to pay the deposit.

After looking at many dresses on the rack, Sofia chose three to try on. The assistant closed the curtains of a wide area and I sat on a small sofa, waiting patiently.

It turned out that the one Sofia really wanted was sold and should have been taken off the rack and she was disappointed. Then the assistant went away and came back with another in a plastic cover.

The curtains closed again, like a theatrical performance, and I waited, and waited, and waited…

Sofia was taking time to look in the mirror on her own, not even the assistant with her, and minutes passed.

As I started to wonder if Sofia had fled the shop through an open window (I know, stupid idea), the curtain opened to a superstar, radiating beauty and with a smile so bright that said, "It's mine!"

Sofia looked fabulous. Despite some adjustments, the dress was exactly as she dreamed of. It was not on the rails as someone else had put it on reserve but had called to say it wasn't for her.

Deposit paid, I took Sofia back to work.

Five days later, we returned to the shop for fitting, and unbeknown to me, some additional flourishes, which explains why it took over an hour, as I spoke to a friend in a nearby park.

On the wedding day, after massage, hair and makeup done, Sofia was breathlessly beautiful in this dress, which is a full-length body-hugging white satin and lace dress, with an open and deep, to the stomach, 'V-neck' of lace, with sleeves of lightly coloured material to blend with the arms, over which is a wider, and flowing translucent white outer-sleeve, which goes to the wrist and finished in white embroidery.

The back was full, with a large heart-shaped panel of the same translucent material and a white fantail of four rounded folds, pinned at the lower back, above the skirt, which, with her outer sleeves billowed and flowed smoothly and easily as we danced.

Sofia's hair was up, pinned by a diamond hairpin and her slippers were skin coloured. Her smile was vibrant, full and radiating happiness. My God! Never was there a more beautiful woman.

Sofia, like most I suppose, kept all her wedding clothes in a special bag, which now hangs lonely in her deserted apartment in Kyiv. It's future far from certain.

Three weeks before the wedding I decided to take Sofia to Bila Tserkva; a town on the way to Odesa, two and a half hours from Kyiv.

Bila Tserkva or 'White Church' as it is called in English, is an ageing, genteel city, with large empty streets and many venerable buildings of historical provenance. I liked the quiet style it had and could easily see its tourist potential if there was money to develop it.

The wide streets and small squares saw the emergence of cafés and restaurants, so its development was starting, albeit too small to be an attraction, simply a service offering. In a store, I spied a light blue T-shirt which I bought, as well as some souvenirs, despite Sofia's sardonic smile.

We walked around the town to the market square, where I made jokes about liking the loud check men's suits and yellow shoes for my wedding attire.

In Bila Tserkva, there is a large park that feels like the great garden of a country house, and it is exactly that, with long winding paths through parkland, man-made lakes with waterfalls and follies in different places. Reminiscent of the setting for the film Sofia so loved, Мой ласковый и нежный зверь.

At the entrance, there were three horse-drawn carriages of the mid-1800s variety, each horse having embroidered headgear.

It was no surprise when Sofia took a great interest in the horses and petted them fondly. I suggested that we take a ride through the park, which we did.

After our ride, we walked around the park to enjoy it, take in the scenery, sit by the lake and waterfall and look at the work of the artists who were painting nearby. There they sat, with trestle and easel, in chosen positions to paint their favoured aspect. Some young, some old… men and women, silently absorbed in the process of making art.

Sofia came with me to buy my suit, not trusting my jokes, and I bought a dark blue suit and shoes in thirty minutes. Usual for me, but disconcerting for Sofia who likes to savour and look at every conceivable option before buying. I wore a white shirt with blue tie, embroidered in the Ukrainian style in light blue silk.

A week before the event, we remembered we needed a master of ceremony, the restaurant organising the DY, and we asked Zoya's friend Denis, who worked in media and had a very calm way about him, if he would do it. This kindly man with great presence agreed. So, all was in hand.

Soon, the day came. Sofia prepared herself at a salon and I prepared at Fortetsa, in the wood house given to us for the day.

I arrived at the events centre early and friends started to gather. Iryna's son was driving Sofia (he has an executive chauffer service and I wanted to keep the money in the family and friends circle) who was traditionally late, well fifteen minutes more than traditional as they went to the wrong door and had to drive round again! Much to my amusement.

There were about forty at the wedding when we went to show the documents again (to triple check), including my longstanding friend Alex, who I rarely see. Alex and I met while I was promoting Irish and Ukrainian business and trade in Ireland while he was consular assistant to Ireland.

When we went to the office, they asked for my residence permit, which I gave them. It was out of date because of the lockdown but the minister had said not to worry until the restrictions had been lifted. Other than a small ten-day window, they remained in place.

There was a problem. We couldn't get married, and they

should call the immigration police and have me deported. WHAT!

Unbeknownst to me, that ten-day window meant I should have renewed the permit, but I didn't know that the window had occurred. Much as we argued, they were certain. I was going to jail.

I asked Alex to help and after some discussion and given everything was arranged, they agreed a ceremony could take place and we would have a mock signing. As long as I agreed to get the resident permit and come back in a few weeks.

The wedding was beautiful, with flowers, smiles and Maria, Aleksandra's daughter, who was two at the time, acting as a flower girl, in a purple dress that she had seen and refused to take off without upset when we went shopping for her.

After the ceremony, we had Champagne and pictures, congratulations from our guests, flowers galore and happy times.

Sofia's friend Iryna's son did the driving to Fortetsa. He had a limousine business, and the large black Audi did the job.

And soon we arrived and waited for our guests, with the Korovai and special embroidery towel, entered the restaurant like a king and queen.

More guests arrived over Champagne and light refreshments and our fabulous photographer Nataliya put us to work. Her brief was to get natural, fun photos with different friends and relatives. She did a superb job; it has to be said.

Despite my direct family and many friends from outside Ukraine being unable to attend due to pandemic restrictions, many Ukrainians close to us did attend, including Svetlana, Sergey, Iryna, Ann and Igor, as well as some of Sofia's extended family, our friends and persons we hold dear to us.

The gifting of presents is a formal process with a long line of people. I am uncomfortable with such kindnesses, but it was really nice. We have many gifts, all special in their own way. Some unique, some intriguing, some personal, all very precious.

Before we ascended to the hall for food and music, I took them to our log house and managed some needed space in peace and quiet.

The meal with about ninety guests went perfectly, although we lost Alex and his family as the baby wasn't feeling well, such a shame.

I made my speech in Ukrainian, having been tutored patiently by Nadiya; a wonderful, patient and caring woman from Irpin who helped me with every word, phrase and intonation.

I wrote the speech and Nadiya translated it into Ukrainian, then polished it as I struggled with a few of the more complex words. This is what I said.

"All our family. All our friends… Thank you!
Galina, Aleksandra, Sasha and Maria, Thank you!

Svetlana, Sergey, Iryna, Gena, Alina, Timofey and Daryna, Thank you!

Sofia, Thank you!

If I remember correctly, we first chatted the day after Sofia's Birthday on February 23rd 2008 (the year of the rat).

It was the 23rd March when we first wrote to each other, having chatted by Skype, often every day. Exactly one month after her birthday. That's over 12 and a half years ago.

On the 11ᵗʰ May, after many conversations on Skype and email, Sofia wrote:

I decided you are in my life when I decided keep in touch with you after your words you will not disappear if I don't want it. I don't want it, but I need to take into account your wishes. I don't know what happen but if you want to keep our contact only in Skype, I respect you desire. If you want to know me better and meet me, I will not resist it. I would like to try. Can I give you some promises now? I think no. We need to meet and spend time together to understand if we can be only friends or more than only friends or nothing. I am not looking for adventures but I'm looking for a man who I can create family. I am not looking for friends because I have them and I thank God for them but if God give me one more, I think it will be expensive gift. But the more important gift would be man who love me and my daughter and who I can build future with, who care of us and who would be farther and husband and friend for us. So, I hope I answered your question. Now I can only wait for your decision.

On the 20ᵗʰ June 2008, we met for the first time at the 5 Camels in Obolon. Many things have changed, but the 5 Camels, Sofia and me remain the same.

There is no doubt that we have lived through many different experiences, some good, some very hard, but lived we did. And to be honest, during the best experiences of my life, Sofia was with me.

Badminton, Yaremche in the snow, the Blue Cave, Kotor,

the journey to Кáм'янéць-Подíльський, Odesa, Hribovka and Roksolany, eating Watermelon even. Each experience inspirational enough on their own, together, they are all a great gift.

None of these are as great as our engagement at Figlmüller in Vienna though. A special event that we both cherish. That was the 16th November 2019.

Sofia and I have been a family for longer than we both know. Not always together, but never far away, if only by messenger or Skype.

In fact, our relationship is like a Ukrainian Oak, slow, but always growing and getting stronger day by day.

As we step forward into new adventures, I know it is for us to make the future, how we want. Of course, no future is interesting without family and without friends, which is why we share our wedding with you today.

Please remember, each one of you have a special place in our hearts and our lives. No matter the distance, no matter the passing of time, you are our family, and we will always need you, always knowing that we are not alone.

So, our family, Thank you!

Sofia, I made my decision and after 12.5 years, (and in another year of the Rat), you are my wife!

Thank you, I am blessed!"

The replying toasts (Sofia opted out due to nerves) made by friends who self-appointed themselves were suitably robust, funny, outrageous and kind. I had water in a vodka bottle and used that to avoid being in an alcohol-induced coma halfway through.

As the speeches came to close, the distinctive guitar

refrain started. It was time for the dance. Everyone looked on, with bated breath. Will Brendan fail at this landmark event? I hoped not.

As we started and moved onward, it was clear it was a hit. There was cheering and claps for the different phases, and the waltz, in such a confined space, was flowing and easy. The lift at the end was a triumph met with a standing ovation and people joining in the dancing.

We had done it! *Phew!*

As we finished, I swapped the vodka bottle of water with one with vodka. Time to celebrate, but not wildly.

Time wore on and soon people started to leave. It was eleven, but Irish weddings last much longer, often going well into the following morning.

Aleksandra and Iryna had words, and Aleksandra and her husband became extremely argumentative. So annoyed was Sasha over their argument that he put his fist through the wall and the unceasing angry words became a scandal.

Despite taking Maria and Aleksandra to the wooden house, the argument persisted, became extremely aggressive, bordering on the physical, and very, very loud, so I suggested that the security guard call the police, in order that they see sense and calm down.

Other people trying to sleep started getting angry and shouting, but at the threat of arrest, Aleksandra and Sasha went home, still arguing at full force as they walked in search of a taxi.

Finally, Sofia and I got to go to bed, on the second floor with the balcony we both admired. As we got upstairs, we saw a lump in the middle…Maria, who had thankfully slept through her parents' rage.

It was the end of a day of many nice things. I wouldn't let it be diminished by other people's behaviours.

The morning was sunny and bright, a repeat of the wedding day, and after breakfast, we started to pack and bring everything, including Maria, to the car.

When we got back to Sofia's apartment, we unloaded. Aleksandra was there, contrite and tried to apologise. I simply said that the argument was part of an Irish wedding... no hassle. But, of course, her verbal aggression was a problem, something that would prove more difficult during war.

After a day's rest, we took Maria with us on our honeymoon to Odesa as Aleksandra was working.

We stayed in an apartment I booked in Airbnb, and we enjoyed walking around the city and walking through the park to the central beaches.

Maria was only two at this stage and after a day at the beach grew tired and irritable because it was hot.

As they walked the twenty minutes from the beach to the apartment, Maria fell asleep, and Sofia lay her on a bench. I had calls to take for potential business and when I rang to meet, Sofia said they were in the park, and she needed help. Maria was heavy!

As I walked through the park trying to find them, I could hear Maria crying. She was loud, very loud, and very insistent.

Taking Maria from Sofia, we walked back... the longest fifteen minutes as Maria broadcast her outrage at not being allowed sleep. Her crying was so loud and desperate that a woman demanded to prove we were her parents and not kidnapping her.

Neither Sofia nor I had time for the woman, and we ignored her, along with others deeply concerned about this wailing, angry child. I have to say though, after we got back to the apartment, I did admire her concern, her civic responsibility and her persistence. Sofia too.

We arrived at the apartment, our walk of shame over and Maria stopped crying. The moment she was lain on the bed, she slept, for over three hours. Thank God!

Our ears ringing from the noise. We had coffee, then a glass of wine. Once Maria was rested, we walked around central Odesa with her and enjoyed the sights, including the horses that people ride on. Sofia and Maria went on a coach ride, while I wandered by myself.

After a few days, we returned to Kyiv.

So, it was a secret. We had a full wedding but weren't married. Only Alex, Svetlana and we knew.

It took two weeks to get the documents and we went back to the wedding service to rebook. The second wedding would be on 23 October 2020!

Our second wedding was a quieter affair with Sofia ditching the dress and wearing a bright red coat as it was cold. Svetlana, Iryna, her daughter, Aleksandra, Maria, Daryna, Sofia's mother and Zoya (Sofia's friend from Childhood) made an all-girl line-up.

The wedding service didn't stint on making the second part of the marriage memorable and we were married in the blue room. Perhaps the only couple to be married in the two rooms, for the same marriage!

After the ceremony, and signing real documents on the altar, we went to a Ukrainian restaurant for a small, but happy celebration.

The day after, we went on our real honeymoon, ten days

to Odesa, Kobleve, Lazurne, Hryhorivka and the salt seas of Liman, Lake Syvash, on the militarised border caused by russian occupation of Crimea, close to Melitopol and Mykolayaiv.

We took Maria with us again, hoping her mood would be better. It was…

Kobleve is similar to Hrybivka and was quiet because we were at the end of the season. Sofia's friend had stayed at the hotel, and we booked there for three days. A modern six-storey hotel with an outside restaurant in the wooded parkland, we had to enter the secure grounds having showed our documents, including Maria's.

Our room was on the ground floor and had a small balcony overlooking two swimming pools. Past the pools lay the silver sands and the Black Sea.

There were few guests in the hotel, certainly not more than forty, so the pools were largely empty and the beach quiet. Perfect for three days of rest for Sofia and Maria, while I explored on foot and had calls relating to possible work.

I really wanted to visit Liman and Lake Syvash, red lakes, saltier than the Dead Sea. Little known but in the previous eighteen months getting some publicity as they had started to use the salty sea muds for cosmetics and some tourism projects had started.

Driving from Hrybivka took us through Mykolaiv and Kherson, past the now legendary Chornobaivka. A very long journey often in unending flat countryside with salt marshes. Not much to see on a very hot sunny day.

We stopped for some money in Luhove; a nice, well-kept, small town. On our way out, I thought I could drive direct, but as I crossed the junction, cars beeped, and a truck driver waived. When I stopped and looked ahead, I could see a massive military block post. They were Ukrainian military guarding the area in case of a further invasion by russian forces occupying Crimea.

Realising I needed to go the whole way round, I didn't know that there were full-scale military exercises involving NATO forces in the area. This made for some interesting scenes, which, even now, cannot be described, as they are covered by Ukrainian martial law, but videos were produced showing massive displays of military techniques, including paratroopers and materiel parachuting from the sky, artillery barrages and warplanes bombing practice targets.

Who knew that eighteen months later, such scenes would be real, with real devastation, losses and hard-to-accept atrocities.

In this part of the world, roads are very long, mostly straight and take ages to get anywhere. The towns are very small settlements and some of them have only rudimentary roads. The countryside is open, often green, with wooded areas and hedges concealing ponds, rivers, fresh and saltwater estuaries, each one teeming with wildlife.

The sign for Lake Lemuria was very hard to see and what was a stoney track, which went for 20km. When we got there, the parking was by a wind farm, with windmills turning slowly in a gently wind. About five cars were stopped there, but it was quiet as we could see people walking out across the vast mud to the shimmering gold waters some distance away.

I drove onto the muddy salt flats and thought we could walk to the sea, as others were doing.

The flats were grey, baked hard in the sun. Where

footprints had been made, they were filled with sharp and long crystals of salt, pure white against the grey, and soft, easily breaking when touched. The ground was warm and smooth. Pretty soon, Maria found a soft patch and was muddy. Now some girls like mud, others no… Maria was a NO! Her cries and discontent simply added to Sofia's scepticism about this vast lonely salt flat that I was fascinated by.

I managed some persistence and with others ahead of us we walked towards the water's edge. It was hot and dry, but the salt air with hot breezes were a joy for me… But me alone.

Small islands of vegetation full of samphire and tall grasses concealed many birds, but they also kept the mud wet and soft, so it was difficult to get too close to the larger ones. I offered both Sofia and Maria some samphire, which is tasty and full of vitamins… they were not impressed.

As we got closer to the water's edge, Maria's wailing was too much for Sofia and she wanted to return to Baby Car.

I have always wanted to see salt flats and look at the nature, but I knew I had reached the limits, so we walked back.

Near where I had parked Baby Car, there was a large pit dug in the mud, with a wooden walkway and steps into the dark pink water. I was keen to try it. Maria was a staunch no! Sofia was a sceptic.

The wood had soft crystals of salt everywhere that water had been splashed, almost like frost, but longer crystals. I was fascinated. Everything was warm like a cosy bath.

I had beach shoes on, and I kicked them off. I was determined to realise a dream and swim in this water and no matter what, I was going to do it. I took off my shirt and went into the water and floated, raised my arms and legs without going under and had fun.

I swam to the middle of the pit, which was about 100 by 200 metres oblong shaped wide and 200m wide and raised my arms and legs at the same time. I expected to go under, but knew that it was possible to float, supported by the high concentration of salt in the water. I DID IT!

Yes, like an upturned turtle, I had legs and arms pointing to the clear blue sky and remained afloat. Wow, wow, wow!

Once out, my antics had been enough to tempt Sofia and she went in. Maria remained unconvinced.

Getting out to be near Maria, as I didn't want any accidents with her falling in, I soon felt dry because of the dry air and hot sun. In fact, Sofia was only in the water for ten mins and by that time I was almost dry.

When we got to Baby Car, she was like an oven; baking hot. We had to open all the windows and the boot to at least get the temperature liveable.

I had read that the nearby village, Novovolodymyrivka, sold salt artefacts… crystals, salt encrusted materials, mud and rock and wanted to go there.

I also wanted to get a big lump of mud from where we were, so as we were waiting for Baby Car to cool down, I dug up about 3kg and put it in a bag. I said to Sofia that properly packaged it was worth over a thousand, but her sardonic smile suggested she really was past caring.

The road to Novovolodymyrivka is little more than a stone track, the best part being the piece between the wind farm that dominated where we had been swimming and the village. Halfway down was a wooden sentry box with a lone security guard who had let us in when we first arrived. As we reached his post, he removed the thin chain from across the road and let a couple of cars in as we left.

It was at this point I began to feel an uncomfortable itch and looking down, noticed my skin was white. Sofia's too… Salt!

The itching was becoming worse as the salt crystals grew on my shorts and T shirt, so we got out and using bottles of water, washed as much of it off as we could.

Feeling better, and a little cooler, I had to brush the seats of the car, as where we sat was also salty, almost like a frost.

The security guard looked at out antics and smiled. We were not the first to stop outside his box to do that and wouldn't be the last.

Reaching the end of the recently stoned track, I turned right into the village. Like so many Ukrainian villages, it was made up of rows of houses in parallel lines.

As I drove slowly to the bottom and then returned on the second row, it became clear that the market wasn't there. In fact, we saw no evidence, save for small wooden benches, which are commonplace in all villages and on roads, where locals sell their homegrown produce, crafts and foraged seasonal foods, such as fruits and mushrooms.

Much as I could have stayed in the area exploring for a couple of days, I had clear indications from my fellow travellers that their tolerance of my idiosyncrasies had reached the limits and a long drive back to civilisation was needed.

From there, I wanted to explore, and Sofia spoke about a very old hotel, чайка (seagull) which was in Лазурне (Lazurne). Sofia was openminded about going and I wanted to explore. A perfect arrangement so!

It took a long time to get to Lazurne, on roads that were made from concrete panels laid on the ground, so Baby Car would *bump, bump, bump,* like a train over tracks. The endless roads seemed much more so, with very little to see other than green hedges, fields and small ponds.

I was very surprised that at the end of this long farm road was a reasonably sized town, full of small hotels, BnBs and shops selling beach ware and food for tourists. It seems that this remote village was popular for tourists, despite the long straight road.

As we drove to the beach, I saw the large sign with a seagull on it and in large letters, the word 'чайка'.

I drove towards what I could see was the beach at the side of the hotel boundary wall and sank in the sand. Baby Car was going nowhere.

Annoyed that we were wheels deep in soft sand, I got out and we went to see the sea and walk to the hotel reception. The beach was busy with families and there were, albeit dated, play equipment and a swimming pool in the tidy, landscaped hotel grounds. The sea was clean, warm and inviting, especially after our salty seadog experiences in Lake Lemuria.

In my experiences in Ukraine, the hotels had been very high standard and here the reception was large and airy, even if it was out of the 1970s.

Being ever the optimist, I suggested we stay two days and we booked. They wanted to be paid upfront, which is not unusual, but something about the expression of the uniformed receptionist (like a flight attendant) caused me to be quizzical.

Returning to Baby Car to move her to the car park, I needed to dig out the sand from under her and, using some flat wood I found, managed to eventually free her. Sofia said nothing but was clearly unimpressed. Maria thought it was fun and Baby Car, being light and manoeuvrable, easily managed to escape once the build-up of sand had been removed from under the wheels, and she had the wood to stop sinking again.

The room we were shown was something out of an abandoned hospital. Plain, simple, one old plug socket and a terrible bath and shower room. It was like a sanitorium, and I said so... Sofia looked at me blankly.

Sofia explained that the hotel was for hospital patients who came for rest in the sea air. It *was* a sanitorium. In my own inimitable, open-minded way, I said, OK... a new experience. Why not!

When we had put our things in the room, we walked past a medical hall and rooms for treatments, which made all the sense in the world. But the sense of being in a hospital began to take form in my brain. I had forgotten that I don't think hospitals are all that comfortable.

We had paid for evening meals, but before then we went for a walk on the sand. Sofia went for a swim.

There is a famous island, Dzharylhach, which is rich in flora and fauna, and I hoped to walk the long spit-like path, some of which is under water, to explore the next day.

When we went to eat, the food was terrible. Old style Hospital food provided in a large hall, and you lined up in a reception area at the appointed time, waiting for a bell that announced they were ready for you. Yes, food was served in shifts, and we were the second.

As we lined up to enter, we got worn coloured trays and walked to the food table, a line of trestles almost.

There was an assortment of grey and colourless foods, mostly overcooked porridge, potatoes and something I didn't recognise, tasteless breaded fried meats, some salads, some fruit and a drink. As I said, hospital food... Yuck!

Most people didn't eat everything and after tasting it, I knew why. Not good. We had to leave at the appointed time and as we did, another group was waiting in the reception area. *Abandon hope all ye that enter there,* I thought. Looking at their pained expressions, I think they knew what was in store.

We decided we would not stay two days and sought to get our money back… with difficulty and a lot of 'but why?', 'there's no reason'. We got some money returned, but not all, then we walked in the hot, dark night.

In the grounds of the car park, I spied walnut trees, and in seconds, Sofia was picking the nuts off the tree… loads of them.

We had no bag, so when I had more than I could carry I went to Baby Car and let them fall into the boot, noisily dropping onto the floor of the boot.

The sound awakened interest from the security guard who came out with his torch… and stayed out.

Sofia was determined to get more and played a game of 'cat and mouse' with the guard. Maria being determined that we would get caught… but no, Sofia insisted that we be her accomplice in this crime and loaded us up with more fresh walnuts.

In the morning, I called the owner of the apartment we used in Odesa, and he agreed that we could stay for two days. Missing breakfast, we left the hotel and sneaked past the guard, who smiled at me, knowing perfectly well what we had been up to.

Hard to think now that these areas are under russian occupation now, with fierce fighting, and that the lives of these people are one of oppression, forced removal to russian camps and death.

Odesa was nice for the remaining days, and we went home to Kyiv satisfied. I even had a lump of salt mud, worth thousands if packaged properly for face packs. It sits in the bathroom of Sofia's abandoned flat in Kyiv.

On our return, I took all our wedding presents to Irpin, for safe storage.

They now sit in dust and debris from russian bombs, far distant from where we are now; in Ireland. Given the upset Sofia feels, I am unsure of their future and how long it will be for me to get them, if I get them at all. So much sadness is attracted by joyful memories.

Chapter 5
Threats of War

After the wedding and honeymoon, I was keen to install the mouldings. They had dried by now and while I still worried about the weight, I had been patient enough.

Petr had agreed to work with me on this and I was glad of this.

Our first challenge was to understand how to do the mitres for the corners. Once this was understood, it was a matter of screws, glue and heavy lifting.

I had bought a machine cutter for the mitres and modified it from its designed use in cutting wood to being able to cut the soft plaster moulding.

The small pieces were no problem cutting-wise, but the large ones were far too big.

Having made all the corners for the small one on my own, it was obvious that it made far too much dust and simply wouldn't work.

We spent the morning trying a few ways, until Petr had a genius idea of creating a template out of wood that would hold the moulding and guide the cut, so it was at forty-five degrees.

By one p.m., we had proven the concept and cut a number of corners, both the left and right sides.

The first day was trial and error and I was pleased it had been successful.

The second day would show if my dreams would be crushed, as everyone told me that they would be, as it was impossible, or I would prevail.

First taking measurements, we marked the walls using templates of both pieces and drew lines, so we knew where to put the lower straight edge. Working the whole day, we marked all the rooms in pencil, with a few adjustments, and started with the smaller flat moulding that would support the bigger contoured piece.

It took us two days to glue and screw (Tec7 is a superb Irish glue that I brought with me, all 41kgs on Ryanair in March 2020), and the most testing piece was the plasterboard walls Dima had built. These were made from single skin plasterboard panels, insulated with soundproofing rockwool. Neither Petr nor I knew if they would take the weight.

Petr had bought some special screws and a hand-held clamping device that made the fixture open out inside the wall to create a large anchor. Once done, we could screw the moulding to the wall, with the requisite glue. It worked!

They were rock solid. Each piece 1m or more long (some were longer than a metre), all rooms were looking good.

The next week, we started with the contoured pieces, which were still very heavy, but maybe forty per cent lighter than they had been.

Because the rooms are old, they aren't square, and alignment was tricky. We developed a technique where the mouldings hung from the ceiling so that they were reasonably straight and of course fully secured.

Once they were aligned, we filled the gaps first with strong foam adhesive, which expanded in the voids to give a good connection between the mouldings and the wall and stopped them from moving.

Then filled the gaps with plaster to allow for a smooth finish for painting.

We took a break over Christmas and on Catholic Christmas Day (25 December), I cooked an Irish Christmas dinner at Svetlana's house, with Sofia, Maria, Svetlana, Sergey, Iryna, her boyfriend Sergey, Petr and his girlfriend Nataliya.

We started the morning with presents, which was a great surprise for Maria, and I cooked both the Irish breakfast, which they abused by adding coleslaw and salad, and the Christmas dinner, which was a full Turkey with sausages inside, ham, roast vegetables, stuffing, which I made (you buy sage at the pharmacist, not the shop in Ukraine, which was new to me), gravy and cranberry sauce which I also made.

It was a lovely day, and we had a really nice few days' rest.

After Ukrainian Christmas, on 7 January, we started back and by the end of January, we were there, except for the filling and sanding smooth.

It looked FANTASTIC!

We had done the impossible and the few pieces that were left were small enough for me to carry and put into the shed. Both Petr and I worried that we would be short, but thankfully, after all the stress, we were done.

Petr decided that the filling and sanding wasn't for him and left me to it.

To be honest, I was exhausted and needed a break, but fortunately Sofia and I had booked to go to Myhove (Migova), a small skiing resort in Chernivtsi region, at the southern end of Hutsulshchyna National Park, some 20km from the

Romanian border.

The very first drive of some distance when we bought Baby Car was to Kam'yanets'-Podil's'kyi, and we passed near it when we drove through Chernivtsi to Myhove.

Kam'yanets'-Podil's'kyi had been our first road-trip in Baby Car. With Sofia, I drove from Kyiv overnight on a hot day at the end of May. I was fascinated to see the famous castle.

The current city was founded in 1062, four years before the famous English battle of Hastings, and believed to have been built on the same place as a city built by the Dacians. In 1241, it was destroyed by the Mongols, and saw Polish, Ottoman, Polish-Lithuanian and russian occupation.

The castle is one part castle and three parts fortress, with fabulous towers of the Disney/Happy Potter kind. The aquaduct over the Smotrych river. It is part of the National Historical-Architectural Sanctuary and one of the one wonders of Ukraine. It is also a candidate for UNESCO World Heritage Site since 1989.

Arriving at six, I drove through the city's modern road in a straight line, through modern parts, buildings of the 50s–90s, then the older architecture, past a park and to a small steep, uneven and cobbled road which went down, twisting as it went.

Being me, I drove slowly and determinedly to the bottom, with houses and trees obscuring and views. At the bottom, the road curved to the left and on the right was a small grassy car park. A narrow green bridge, suitable for only one person, both ways, in line crossed a shallow river and ahead was an ancient church. Dominating above us were the castle ramparts.

As I parked the car and opened the window, a cockerel crowed its welcome. We had arrived.

Both of us were soon asleep, and remained so till after nine thirty, despite locals walking past the open window to cross the bridge to visit the church and for children to play at an adjacent playground.

It was a hot morning and even though it was early, we were awake.

As the sun bore down, we crossed the narrow wooden bridge using the metal rails for balance and entered a grassy flat area where a beautiful wooden church hides under the castle walls.

Zdvyzhens'ka Tserkva, is a three-storeyed wooded church that is really enchanting. Dominated by the castle walls and a huge cliff on the opposing side, this old church has little information written about it.

All I can say it that it is definitely worth a visit.

The church is all wood, including the rooftiles, and sits on a base of square-cut stones. There's a bench for sitting on and a playground to one side.

Exploring under a clear blue sky with a hot sun was easy, peaceful and relaxing. Returning over the river Smotrych was calm, happy and greatly cherished.

We then motored back up the steep windy lane to the top, I was stuck by the number of vehicles that passed this way… what I thought was a much-neglected laneway served quite a few houses. Once back on the asphalted road, I turned left and towards the famous aqueduct.

As we approached the aqueduct, the castle sat above us, serene and yet powerful, its round towers majestic. Honestly, Disney took his ideas from such places. Later, I would learn that there is a hot air balloon festival here and the pictures of many, very large, colourful and unusual hot air balloons hovering over the castle skyline are spectacular.

The aqueduct stands high above the river and the views are fabulous. Once over the steep river valley, the solid ancient walls of the castle dominate, their yellow stone walls inviting and safe.

I parked Baby Car and we walked around to the main gate, which is an impressively large arch in the wall. Paying the small fee, you enter a large open expanse where some re-enactors showcase medieval life. Usual enough, I guess, but the openness and relaxed informality was very encouraging.

Once inside the castle, you are free to roam, and we did. The towers are made of the same yellow stone and topped by conical tiled roofs with a pennant flying from delicate flagpoles. The roof sits on a red brick base and each one has narrow winding stairs to the top.

As with all fortifications, the spaces created for firing weapons made for intriguing viewing points as you ascend. There are wooden floors that had a variety of uses, with the last one acting as foundation for the large wooden structures that formed the cone of the roof.

From the openings, we could see the different terraces which would once have been used for food production in case of siege and attacks. No doubt people would have lived in small wooden houses there also.

At the back of the castle, you can see a large gap in the fortified wall, where larger horse-drawn vehicles could enter the enclosure. Behind the gate was a stone-built armoury and rooms for cannons etc., distant from the castle, but within the enclosure.

What was certain is that this castle was built for defensive strength and its longevity was testament to the success of its architects.

After several hours exploring, keeping out of the hot sun and enjoying the cooler air in the towers and buildings, we sat for some very tasty shashlik, which is either seasoned chicken or pork cooked over wood and some very refreshing Uzvar, which is made from smoked and dried fruits, apples, pears, plums, boiled in water and served cold.

Both these are traditional Ukrainian food and really, really tasty.

We sat outside where there were wooden tables, soaking up the atmosphere and watching the re-enactors showcase life from previous times.

Such a nice afternoon.

We walked the aqueduct to see the views then drove back to the other side.

Between the church and the castle are many old squares, cobbled streets and interesting buildings so we went there to explore. We walked around several small squares, one of which had a small market selling crafts, souvenirs and local produce, like honey, fruits and cheeses.

As we idled the late afternoon away, we came upon a house on a narrow street where a sign advertised rooms for rent. Sofia called and the gate was opened by a woman who beckoned us in.

€20 for a double room ensuite for the night! That's a done deal.

We moved Baby Car to the narrow, cobbled street on which the three-storey modern house stood and brought our things. After a sleep and a shower, we were ready for the evening.

Ukrainians love coffee shops; in fact, a Ukrainian war hero and member of an ancient Ukrainian Cossack family named Yuri Kulczyk brewed the first cup of coffee in Vienna, sometime after the Battle for Vienna in 1683, in a place called 'Under the Blue Bottle'.

He did so because his successes in battle were rewarded with Turkish coffee beans, which he used.

Yuriy was born in 1640 and was a merchant who began his career as a translator. He was fluent in Turkish, Serbian, Hungarian, Romanian and German. Later, he sold carpets, silk, gold and silver, while remaining a Turkish translator at the court of Austrian Emperor.

During the Turkish Siege of Vienna, he expressed great wit and courage to fight the enemy, and volunteered to leave the besieged and starving city to bring forces that would free it from the Turks.

He left the city in Turkish attire and crossed enemy lines. Knowing perfectly not only Turkish but Turkish customs, he successfully fulfilled his mission.

The grateful townspeople of Vienna offered a reward, as you do, but were very surprised when he asked for the trophy bags of coffee that no one wanted to take, instead of the offered gold.

At that time, everyone in Austria believed that blue-green grains were just simply food for camels. Kulczycki knew that these grains were used for preparing a favourite Turkish drink, coffee.

In addition to three hundred bags of coffee, Yuriy received from the emperor a commemorative silver medal, Viennese citizenship, a house in the Austrian capital, and the right to open the first coffee house in Vienna.

This Ukrainian started the first coffee business in Europe.

At the beginning, he wore Turkish attire, distributing coffee on Vienna's streets. But very few people in Europe knew about coffee and the price was very high. His innovation to serve coffee with milk and sugar, to lower the price and sweeten the deal, attracted more and more people, founding the global tradition we see today.

His abilities, character and personality helped popularize coffee in Austria and in time, his café became one of the most popular places in the town.

Each of the cafe's visitor was greeted with the affectionate words "bratchyku-serdenko" ("brother-darling"). This Ukrainian expression for a long time could be heard in the Viennese dialect, even though it was very definitely a foreign import.

In a large room of the newly built Kulczycki's coffee-house, there were wooden tables and benches that were modelled on Ukrainian house interior designs.

The host served the guests alongside his beautiful wife wearing magnificent Ukrainian national dress, that attracted even more attention from the visitors.

Today's visitors to Vienna, including us when we went for our engagement, can visit Kulczycki-Gasse Street.

There are many coffee shops in Kam'yanets'-Podil's'kyi, and the old buildings, cobbled streets and relaxed atmosphere makes them really attractive, but we wanted to eat and drink some wine.

Ukrainian wine is very good quality, and we were near Moldova and Romania, so there was great choice from all three great wine countries. We sat in a large comfortable restaurant, very French in some ways, and relaxed. Perhaps too much.

Soon it started to rain, and a thunderstorm rattled the green canopies outside the big restaurant windows. Two of the staff brought in the chairs and tables from outside and closed the canopies, returning inside, fully drenched and dripping. Smiling in that bemused way one does.

The storm was magnificently dynamic, as many are in mountainous regions. The dark of the night boomed and flashed as we had a few more drinks. But the signs were clear. The restaurant was closing, and we needed to leave. As we said our goodbyes, lighting and thunder was near simultaneous overhead and even the ground shook...*BOOM!*

Running the 1km distance was fun, as I somewhat drunkenly claimed I was running between the raindrops and other stupidities, but we soon got to the house. The evidence of my failings as a runner between the raindrops was clear in the morning when our clothes, that we threw in wildly after we returned from dancing through the storm, sat in a puddle of water. Downstairs near the front door, we were soon to learn the fate of our shoes. A very unpleasant cold wet experience to be avoided if you can!

We walked a little then decided to go to a small café for breakfast. As we left our accommodation, I reflected on the adventure that we were having, so cool.

The café was like many in Ukraine; clean, airy and full of funny, curious books, bits of bikes, photos of people being happy. As it was sunny and warm, we sat outside on the stone pavement at the edge of a cobbled street for omelette and coffee.

Before we drove for home, we walked the old streets past

an ancient church and some fortified building, outside of which were a group of tourists, teenagers really, and their guide.

Somewhere, someone was playing a bass, creatively and elegantly; the sounds drafting from windows, many of which had wooden shutters, open, half open and closed. This was a cool place.

After about an hour, we headed off for Khmelnitsky and Kyiv.

By March 2022, Kam'yanets'-Podil's'kyi would gain world attention for hosting four hundred and seventy Indians and many other foreign students, seeking escape from russian invaders, via Romania.

In February 2021, we were off to Myhove, driving through a freezing cold night and arriving in the morning. I thought about stopping again in Kam'yanets'-Podil's'kyi, which was two hours from Myhove, but decided Chernivtsi was better. In any case, I wanted to see the famed university.

It was bitterly cold in Baby Car, even with the full heating on, ice formed on the window edges, inside!

Multiple coats, ski clothes, boots and blankets were needed and even then, it was a hard drive.

Sofia went to the back seat and buried herself under the blankets. I drove, sternly and persistently. I like driving and there's plenty of space in my head for thinking over things.

By the time we arrived in Chernivtsi, we had stopped a few times to warm up and we were tired. When we parked at the corner of the main boulevard, the snow was piled half a metre high. First, we slept a little.

We decided to go to a hotel on the corner as it was open for breakfast and we were pleased for the warmth, the toilets and hot food.

We relaxed and ate, spending our time resting, not speaking much. Sofia had been quiet, but she can be that way, as can I. We both live in our heads a lot.

It was a nice breakfast and we decided to drive and find the university, because it was too damned cold to walk!

Chernivtsi is a beautiful city of wide streets. The jewel in the crown though is undoubtedly 'Yuriy Fedkovych Chernivtsi National University built for the Metropolitan (a bishop equivalent, I guess) of Bukovina, Roman Orthodox Church and designed by the Czech Architect Joseph Glavka and built from 1864–1882.

Unlike other world class universities, it avoided the oppressive power expressions of baroque or gothic styling and draws from Byzantine and Romanesque architecture, with a roof with icing white like tracing using white tiles.

It's small and almost delicate. In summer, the well-laid gardens and interesting interiors would be great to explore, but it was freezing, so all we did was look from Baby Car... promising a return when there's heat in the sun.

Myhove is about one and a half hour's drive from Chernivtsi, through good roads.

The turn for Myhove off the dual carriageway is a turn into country roads, small villages and farmland.

It was really beautiful in the thick white snow, and we could see the mountains of the Vyzhnytsia National Park, which is part of the colossal Carpathian Mountains that sit astride the Ukraine, Poland and Romanian borders.

Truly, the vast beauty of this area is special... and we were staying for a week.

The village of Myhove has done a great job in creating a

114

small family ski resort with two ski runs and the usual arrangement of restaurants, hotels, ski hire shops and souvenir market. Absent any massive hotels or nightclubs, it is for enjoying the scenery, nature and snow sports.

It sits at the end of the village with a forestry road continuing far into the mountains. Certainly not a route for long-distance travel, but important for the houses, villages and settlements where the local people live.

Out hotel was on the opposite side from the ski runs, up a very steep single-track road, lined with wood houses, chalets and wooden restaurants.

Where we were staying was at the very top and as we arrived at the ski runs, we were directed to a car park next to the mostly frozen river. From there, we were taken up on a quad bike... bags stuffed into the back shelf and bouncing as we raced at speed.

Arriving at the reception in less than three minutes, we were refreshed and completely restored by the cold air. We were shown to our rooms, which were wood-lined, consisting of hall, bathroom, bedroom, dinner/kitchen room.

Both the bedroom and dining room were open plan, each having a balcony from which to see the commanding views. Below the balcony was a small outside swimming pool that was closed, and underneath was the indoor pool, massage rooms and sauna.

At the front was the restaurant and bar, which had even better views of the spectacular scenery.

As was usual, I had brought treats and laid them out on our table. Sofia's favourite, Kyivsky Tort from Roshen, sweets, fruit, some wine, cognac and nuts, but for some reason, Sofia lacked interest.

She was quiet, wordless and pre-occupied.

The following day, we had breakfast on the glazed terrace overlooking the valley and the heavily forested mountains. It was yoghurt with fruit jam, omelette with salad, some bread and cheese, coffee and blinchiky (pancakes) with cream and jam.

It was nice and we were tired, so Sofia used her voucher for a massage and swim. I decided to walk outside and explore. Little happened till late afternoon when we walked down to the ski centre to get equipment.

Tired from putting up the mouldings, I opted out of skiing, but Sofia went. Unusually, she didn't ski much although seemed happier.

The second day, we went and explored the small shops and markets, buying a sheepskin rug and a large, thick, long-haired wool blanket in a traditional design for using in Baby Car on the way back.

As Baby Car was safely parked, we decided to use her for storage and walked back up to the hotel, after having some Glintwein, hot wine with spices, popular in cold countries.

The following day, I used my voucher for a massage and explored the forests in the mountains, struggling in the deep snow and in awe of the absolute natural beauty all around, while Sofia was skiing.

It was clear Sofia was deeply unhappy and by the third day, it was about to pop… I am not someone who allows things to fester and an unhappy person in an idyllic setting made no sense.

We had decided to walk along the road away from the village and into the mountains. This road was flat and followed the river.

There were few buildings and a small sawmill at the side of a forester's college, which could house no more than thirty students at a time.

We walked for maybe 15km in silence, Sofia going on ahead with a puppy which had emerged from under a wooden picnic platform and decided to join us.

Soon Sofia was out of sight and so I explored by myself, ignoring the sense of grievance that we were having unshared experiences in a beautiful place.

I returned alone and after about two hours decided to drive to find her. Really, this is big wild country and it's not a place to get lost. I drove 10km then returned, as the track was difficult for Baby Car, and I feared getting stuck. No sign of Sofia.

As I returned to the wooden platform, I saw Sofia with the two puppies, and I stopped. She was happily playing with the puppies but said nothing to me. I waited fifteen minutes and said I would meet her back at the car park. She returned about an hour later and we silently went for something to eat.

This was miserable, but I didn't want any upset. We walked silently up the mountain road to the hotel, taking in the multitude if stars in a black sky. Nothing took Sofia's interest.

On returning to her room, she took to the bed, declining any of the treats I had brought. That was enough. I needed to speak.

I don't know what was wrong and I perhaps never will, but she was upset and deeply unhappy with life. It was a difficult night, but like a storm in the night, the morning saw Sofia feeling better, happier and talking again. *Phew.*

The next few days were much better as we explored. Sofia went skiing, with a bit more happiness showing and I used the dinghy slide (a large rubber donut sliding down what is like a toboggan run) which was fun.

When we left Myhove, I was impressed with what they were trying to do and the quality of the experience, which was very cheap. €25per day BnB incl., of breakfast for two.

We left at about eleven a.m. and headed for Khmelnitsky first. We stayed there for a couple of hours for lunch and a walk around the large central square then returned to Kyiv.

As we left, I wondered about returning to Khmelnitsky at another time. Not realising that in a year we would be in a safe house as sirens warned of cruise missiles and rocket attacks.

A few days later, I took the blanket, sheepskin rug and the many souvenirs to Irpin, as Sofia wanted her flat free from clutter. I placed them with the wedding presents and shared their fate.

We got back to Kyiv on the 21st in the evening and life settled down. On the 26th, I had installed the bathroom cabinet, drilling through a cable while I did it. Fortunately, I found an electrician who did a work around, otherwise the new tiles would have to be removed to repair the cable and that would have been a disaster.

Sofia had bought a new chair, a blue and green bean bag and a table for her flat, which seemed a little odd, but she was happy, which was the main thing.

The snows were melting but I went alone to the forest on 6 March, where it remained in pockets. Life was pottering along, although for the third month Gena had failed to pay money he owed.

I had loaned Gena money and he repaid me every month, with a few explainable hiccups. By April, I was concerned as his promises failed to materialise. I learned that he had given

118

the money to someone else, and they reneged on paying. I was annoyed. This money was to support me during the pandemic months of not working and having no money was serious. I had enough until July.

Prospecting for work was ongoing, speaking with CEOs and SVPs of corporations and large businesses. We always got good responses, but no work. They simply didn't want consultants as people were working from home.

I filled the time with proposals, walking around the lake and forest. But money was a growing issue.

There were some opportunities that we invested heavily in, but something always frustrated the opportunity. I would get bits and pieces of money from Gena when he had some, but it was irregular and unreliable.

Through spring and summer, I explored around Irpin, Dmitrivka, Vorzel, Bucha, Hostomel and Horenka in Baby Car, as Sofia had lost interest, I am happy in my own company so that was OK. In summer, Sofia went to Turkey with Aleksandra and Maria, which suited me. I stayed in Irpin, more and more.

In August, Baby Car was damaged by bad fuel and needed major work. Svetlana gave me back some money I had given her some years previously when she had bought the house and that almost covered the bill. In the meantime, Sofia and I went to Chernivtsi for the day.

Driving through the forests and fields to Chernivtsi was nice, but very long. Hidden in the forest is a large military training base which you had to drive through and then the road was empty of anything, other than trees.

A few villages did spring up and I was worried about fuel. We stopped at a sawmill, and they sent us down a narrow lane to a small wooden village. We actually passed the village and found a military town with many houses. There, they explained, we couldn't get fuel, but the village had a tyre replacement shop where it was possible.

The roads to and through the village were simply sand and all the houses were old, made up of wood blackened by age.

We stopped and asked an old man on a bicycle and he pointed to a cluster of wooden houses and sheds. When we got there, a man came from behind a wooden door and soon gave us a 10l can of fuel.

Fuelled up, we travelled to Chernivtsi, barely making it.

We parked in the centre of town and went for a walk after having coffee and a cake.

It was 13 August and Sofia was happy. Not her usual self, but happy. The sun shone as we walked to the church at the bottom of the very wide central avenue. We sat overlooking the dual carriageway connecting Belarus to Kyiv, little imagining that a 60km russian military column would fill this highway, a little over six months later.

In September, I went mushroom collecting with friends in the forest and later went with my cousin Christopher to Dmitrivka to do the same.

Christopher is a musician and teacher. He was living in Kyiv and had produced his own opera. A modern one that I was obligated to watch… It's good! I said.

I took him to a Ukrainian village restaurant, and he enjoyed playing a bandura or kobzar, a traditional Ukrainian string instrument which looks like a cross between a guitar and a Turkish oud.

Catholic Christmas was sent at Sofia's flat. New year 2022 was quiet, but we took Maria to Sophieska Square and Kontraktova Ploshcha to see the massive Christmas tree, lights and funfairs on 5 January. On the 29th, I took Maria to play in the snow and walk along the River Dnipro in Natalka Park, a beautiful park created by the city administration of Vitaly Klitschko.

Despite money worries, things were unusual, and we booked to go skiing again, this time to Dragobrat in early March.

Unbeknown to us, we would be fleeing russian forces then.

Vladimir Putin has harboured hatred of Ukraine and Ukrainians for a very long time, for many reasons well publicised, but driven by historical loathing reaching back hundreds of years, a demographic reality in russia that, unless altered, would see a collapse in the country into a number of new republics.

I wrote a piece in 2014 about the logic Putin had to eradicate Ukrainians and populate Ukraine with russians to build a large western territory, so that in the event of a collapse, the much-reduced russia, which would absorb Belarus and Ukraine, would stretch from the Baltic to the Black sea. From St Petersburg to Yalta.

This territory would be big enough in size and population to retain russia's position in the G8 and the United Nations.

Publishing this piece attracted the attention of some russian heavy hitters, including Zhirinovsky, a hate-filled man who died in the early part of the russian invasion in 2020.

By autumn 2021, incremental menacing by russia and its political elites was increasing and while not a topic of ongoing conversation, came up from time to time.

In November and December, things were heating up in terms of large assemblies of military technology, troops and rhetoric.

121

Chapter 6
Documents, Damned Documents

The email on 25 January from the Irish Embassy in Kyiv finished with a clear statement.

'...please note that there are currently no plans to evacuate Irish Embassy staff or their families from Ukraine.'

A second follow-up email included the comment, *'we do not wish people to panic'.*

Despite all the talk, Ireland, which is a member of the UN Security Council and has access to the most accurate intelligence data did not view the gathering military forces on the Ukrainian border as an immediate threat. Other Embassies had the same position.

This was one month before the invasion began.

Life with Sofia was getting difficult as she continued being introverted. I had seven a.m. calls twice a week and to avoid any disturbances, it suited me to live in Irpin on those days, returning when I wasn't busy, sometimes to collect Maria from kindergarten. This was a far cry from before, but life can be like that.

I love being in Irpin anyway and despite the cold weather outside, my apartment was warm, if unfinished. In myself, I was calm.

On the 31st, the embassy emailed to invite me to an online call with the Ambassador Therese Healy on 2 February, at five p.m.

On that call, the ambassador made it clear that Ukrainian family members needed visas to enter Ireland and that paperwork was necessary. I expressed my concerns that this was time-consuming, expensive and had difficulties, because visas were processed in Moscow.

This situation led to many strange refusals, including a seventy-year-old refused because they may seek to work illegally in Ireland!

Over twenty years, I had seen very many complaints about Moscow and had brought my own personal experiences to the secretary general, who did initiate some changes. To be clear, having the visas processed in Moscow was a disaster. To describe this, I used the example of English people in London processing Irish visas to the US during what many call 'the Troubles'. You can imagine the rest.

I was to find out later that the waiting list at this time was over nine hundred.

Ireland's position on visas for Ukrainians was out of step with other member states in Europe. All the others were visa-free, either due to Schengen or bilateral agreements for three months.

As the UK had left the EU, this anomaly stuck out for me.

The EU had agreed to introduce a standard visa application process similar to the US ESTA card. This was planned to commence at the end of 2022 and is called ETIAS.

The new Minister of Justice, Helen McEntee, is a young professional, who in December 2021 had moved to change arrangements for southern African countries and on 31

January, had introduced an amnesty for seventeen thousand undocumented living in Ireland.

It seemed to me that this minister, having demonstrated her courage in changing these restrictions, was potentially open to changing visa free to include Ukrainians.

On 4 February, I saw a post from a man called Dave on Irish Supporters of Ukraine, asking for help with the visa situation as he was married to a Ukrainian and she had family in Ukraine. I immediately offered to help as it triggered my current thinking into action.

I had a call with Dave and then drafted a letter to Minister McEntee for discussion. He liked the draft and with two Ukrainians living in Ireland, Anna and Natasha, we had a number of calls to align.

What I was suggesting was a direct approach, not a campaign, based on a factual letter and supported by twenty senior figures with unimpeachable reputations with connections between Ukraine and Ireland. These would be both Irish and Ukrainian nationals.

I was pleased that they agreed about a direct approach, because many public campaigns go nowhere, often because they attract disruptive people who do more harm than good, dragging messages along a bumpy road of animus and political enmity.

By 14 February, the letter with signatures was done. Twenty signatures, including people from the EBRD, business, academia, medicine and religion. No politicians, as I planned, although there were some ready to sign. I just didn't want this to be a political football. I saw the change on visas as a technical one. Without this change, the ETIAS system would not work the same in Ireland as for other countries, making it far more complicated than necessary.

In the lead up to finalising the letter, Dave, Anna and Natasha were trying to get an audience with Minister McEntee, but this was proving difficult.

On the 12th, the Irish Embassy wrote another email;

I am emailing to notify you of a significant change to our travel advice for Ukraine. Based on the security situation in Ukraine, we are now advising against all travel to Ukraine. Furthermore, we advise those currently present in Ukraine to leave as soon as you can.

This was clarified in a call. Leave Ukraine now.

It was clear to me that they meant Irish people, not their families. The effect would be an abandonment of family members and I wasn't going to do that. No way. How could I live with myself? I couldn't.

Feeling the immediacy of events, I unilaterally reached out to a local politician. I needed to escalate.

On the 14th, I reached out to my local councillor representing the Cooley mountains in Ireland, Antoin Watters.

Antoin and I know each other but not well. I had done some work on a website for his employer and we maintained contact. When he sought political office, I supported him. He is really a very capable and dedicated local representative. I messaged him on Facebook asking for help at about six p.m. Irish time.

He answered quickly and explained. His answer was quick and simple. "I will get Ruairí to call you, tomorrow."

Ruairí Ó Murchú is an elected representative to Dail Eireann, the Irish parliament. A young progressive, dedicated to Ireland and his local constituents, he was unstinting in his support, calling me regularly during the arduous journey that lay ahead, not that I knew about it at that time.

He called on the 15th due to Dail commitments, and I explained what I was trying to do and sent him the final draft. His response was simple.

"I will see the minister tomorrow and will hand it to her."

Perfect! There can be no denial of receiving the letter and she would know that it will be of public interest, subject to a follow up in Dail Eireann. No civil servants involved. I sent him the finished document in scanned form.

At the same time, I was trying to get money from Gena and maintain some connection with Sofia.

Valentine's Day did not go well. I had bought some presents, but I also had a call in the morning, so I left her gifts on a table. She was deeply unhappy that I did that, and no explanation about being on a call would be accepted.

In my defence, Sofia had said many times that Valentine's Day is expensive and it's better to do something on a later day, a few days or so afterwards, and in previous times she bought presents also. Not this year. The rift was getting larger. Whatever was driving her remoteness, it was becoming unpleasant. Sofia's refusal to talk about things doesn't help.

You simply have to keep living.

On the 15th, I followed up with Ruairí about getting documents, the most difficult being for Daryna, Sofia's mother-in-law and Aleksandra's grandmother.

Daryna is eighty and has never had an international passport. Her red passport is decades old, possibly forty years, but certainly before 1990.

Demand for appointments had gone sky high, made more so as many offices were closed due to covid infections. The only option was to book online at an independent express service, immediately after twelve at night. Sofia tried several times, but it was booked out even minutes after twelve.

They also explained it would take one month at the earliest to process any documents, which then had to be translated into English and stamped by an Apostille, which is a government stamp to prove authenticity.

We were easily five or six weeks away from having the documents to submit with the visa application.

Sofia managed to get a booking for the 18th, but Daryna was very stressed and upset. Government upset her and the whole idea of travelling out of Ukraine was torture. She had been in hospital three times over the last six months, with pneumonia and covid.

When I went to pick her up for the appointment, she was collapsed, crying on the floor. She was in a panic, she couldn't go. To see an eighty-year-old so distraught was immensely difficult and I knew that she simply needed more time.

I called Sofia to explain and went to Irpin.

Sofia called the office, and they gave her a new date. 24 February.

On 18 February, the ambassador emailed again.

'If you are still in Ukraine, our strong advice very much remains that you leave as soon as possible. Do not delay.'

In bold! This meant, abandon my family. I WILL NOT DO THAT!

I sent the email to Ruairí… He went to the minister and to the departments of justice and foreign affairs. Their response, 'We are working in this'.

On Monday, 21 February, Ruairí asked if I would talk to the media. I happily said yes… he sent out a statement saying that the government needed to come up with a workable solution on the basis of the situation.

The government issued a statement saying they would process visa applications without delay. The backlog of nine hundred was gone… all of a sudden!

But this didn't help me, nor many others.

That same day, Putin recognised the occupied territories in Donbass and started moving russian troops in.

That same day, the Irish Times called. Ruairí had given them the number. This piece would light a fuse and throughout the day I had calls from journalists in print, radio and TV.

On 22 February, media interest was spiking, I was on radio and TV. The Irish Times piece had done its job and I was grateful. I will also say that all the journalists and editors were superb. No limitations, say what you have to say… On radio and TV, it's your slot. I will be forever grateful for that.

Both Ruairí with the government and me in the media generated huge public interest, including where I live in Ireland. The regional radio station LMFM booked a call for two p.m. Irish time on the 23rd.

Later that day, the embassy emailed again.

First and foremost, I would like to stress that if you are still in Ukraine, our strong advice remains that you leave immediately and without delay.

On the 23rd, the embassy emailed again;

As has been communicated, the Department of Justice are prioritising Ukrainian visa applications for spouses/dependants of Irish citizens. The normal waiting times do not apply. If you apply online and send us the application number, the embassy can bring it to the attention of the Department of Justice for prioritisation. The circumstances in Ukraine at the moment are of course highly unusual, and this is certainly being taken into account in visa decisions.

Also note that you do not need all the paperwork to be in place at the time of making the online visa application on the Department of Justice website: (www.irishimmigration.ie), – the supporting documents can be submitted after. The sooner you apply online, the faster the visa can be issued.

On the evening of the 23rd, the embassy called me, asking what my situation was. I answered, "No different." They suggested they were looking at options but were concerned I was still in Ukraine.

I explained again my situation. I had no documents for Daryna and I told them about her collapsing, they were sympathetic and asked me to register. As it was late in the evening, I said I would do it in the morning. On 24 February 2022.

The day Russia escalated the war and attacked Hostomel, Irpin and Bucha.

At 12.15, Ruairí messaged me saying the minister was looking for him to get a copy of our letter, seeking visa-free arrangements… she had lost it.

At 15.24 on the 24th, the embassy emailed again.

In light of developments, we advise you to shelter in a secure place at this moment in time. Keep your situation and any travel plans under constant review and ensure your travel documents are up to date.

However, you could consider leaving Ukraine if you judge it safe to do so, depending on your location and prevailing circumstances.

It is likely that routes out of Ukraine will be severely disrupted, and the road network and border crossings may face closures at short notice. Martial law has been declared in Ukraine, and the airspace is closed. You should closely monitor the advice of local authorities and reputable media sources. Bear in mind that communication lines (phone, internet) may be disrupted.

After a further call, they emailed again.

Dear Brendan,

Further to our phone conversation this afternoon, the number for our dedicated emergency consular assistance telephone line is <u>01-6131700 (a Dublin number)</u>.

As mentioned, please be aware that the capacity of our Embassy to provide consular assistance is extremely limited at the present time.

Ireland's government were in a panic. I was being pursued by many journalists and the Minister for Foreign Affairs made a statement that there would be a process. What that would be,

130

he couldn't say.

Minister Coveney's advisor Fiachre Kelly called me for an update. It was simple. We were at war and in incredible personal danger.

On the morning of the 25th, the Taoiseach, Michael Martin made a statement to press on the steps of Dail Eireann. The Minister of Justice will make a statement.

Around 12.00, Minister McEntee made her statement.

"The Minister for Justice Helen McEntee TD has announced the immediate lifting of visa requirements for Ukrainian citizens travelling to Ireland.

This will streamline and support the swift exit of both the Ukrainian family members of Irish citizens, and the family members of people from Ukraine who are resident in Ireland.

It will apply as an emergency measure to all Ukrainians travelling to Ireland.

The Statutory Instrument removing the visa requirement for Ukraine nationals as an emergency measure takes immediate effect.

Ukrainian citizens who are considering leaving Ukraine and travelling to Ireland may for the coming period do so without a visa if they judge it safe to travel. Those Ukrainian citizens who travel to Ireland without a visa during this period will then have ninety days after arrival to regularise their position. This position will be kept under ongoing review with the impact monitored closely."

Dave called me, very happy. I replied that it was too late. I had failed. I meant it... it was too late for flying to Ireland and being five hours from Kyiv to Tullaghomeath. Now we had to take the country road, taking weeks.

Now, millions of Ukrainians, up to fifteen million, I estimated, correctly, would be on the move away from war, in distress and panic. The window of opportunity for composed and calm travel lost.

My job now was to escape. With Daryna, Sofia, Aleksandra, Maria, Tosha the cat and Lisa the dog. By car. A journey that would take fifteen days, the first ten being under threat of death.

Chapter 7
Russia Attacks

It was the morning of the 23rd and I went to collect Daryna for her biometric passport interview.

When I arrived, she was slumped on the floor, Lisa sitting beside her, the gate and the door of the flat both open. Such was the panic and distress that I worried that Daryna was going to have a medical emergency. There was no question, Daryna was not going to the meeting.

This small, frail eighty-year-old woman lying on the floor, almost like dirty clothes by the washing machine, save for the sobbing and cries of despair.

"Brendan! Brendan! I can't, please, I can't go. Let me rest."

Having settled her into her apartment, I drove to Irpin, calling Sofia at work and explaining the situation. The reality was that the demands for documentation brought Daryna to the brink. The window was closed, at least for now.

I decided to stay in Irpin for a few days. I had work to do, some early calls that disturbed everyone and it suited me.

Pokrovska Street had new lights and as the early evening drew in, the outlines of the tree-lined street took on a much-loved ethereal air.

Opposite, the small shop Alenka! was busy as usual. A constant stream of people dropping in for a chat and the few essentials they needed. Bread, cheese, milk, toilet paper, biscuits, alcohol, coffee. You know.

Greatly appreciated for the warmth of the welcome and standing outside chatting, despite of the weather, the magic of Alenka was never lost on me.

As time passed, I readied for bed.

It was 21.45 when my phone rang.

Brendan! It's Dima, you need to leave Irpin. There will be an attack and we think it will be tonight or early morning.

I immediately called Sofia.

"Hi, where are you?"

"I'm at home with Maria, why?"

"Call Aleksandra, tell her to come straight to you after work, we need to leave."

"Now?"

"Yes."

"OK."

Forty minutes later, I was in the flat in Obolon. Bags had been packed but Aleksandra was defiant.

"No! I will not go. This is hysteria! Who said this? No, I will stay. Tomorrow, I want to work in the restaurant. I am not going.

"OK," I replied, "we will go with Maria and if anything happens, get a Taxi to Svetlana's house. OK?"

We then went to Daryna. Asleep, she was disturbed by Sofia who got her things and brought her to the car. Very frail and confused, she simply did as she was told. Like an obedient child.

We got to Svetlana's in thirty-five minutes and soon settled in. Shortly afterwards, we slept.

The morning broke to silence. Nothing.

After breakfast, Sofia asked to go to work and that I return Daryna and Maria to Obolon.

On our return, I filled the car with as much gas as physically possible. Filling a ten-litre can as well.

The day passed as usual, no recriminations and at eleven p.m., we went to bed.

As I slept, I heard the first missiles. *Boom, Boom, Boom, Boom!* Sirens and alarms rang out. Ambulances and fire trucks filled the streets. Five thirty a.m. That's when it started.

It was 24 February and war was here.

I closed all the curtains in case of glass breaking and asked everyone to be calm. Have coffee, a shower and re-pack the bags. We will not rush, and we will not travel into unknown danger.

I decided to wait, just so we could understand where was safe.

It was about eight twenty when I took the first bags to the car. It was a still morning and others were silently filling cars. No words spoken, which was unusual.

A young woman was desperately trying to get a taxi to another part of the city. She anxiously asked if I could take her. With five adults, a dog and a cat, it was impossible.

The tears in her eyes, the stiff shaking of her body told me she was breaking inside. I had no cure. No one had. The realisation she was on her own was stark and appalling, but what could I do? I felt desolate. There was no opportunity for heroism, and it was highly possible that taking a chance for her would mean abandoning my family. Not knowing where was safe, it could have been a death sentence.

I was emotionally empty and incapable as I watched her pensive, pacing and trying to get through to people on her phone. I hope she is safe.

As we picked up Daryna, she was again subdued and confused. For me, I had to focus. What took forty minutes on the 22nd took four hours.

Returning to PetrPavlBorshegovka and Svetlana's house, we de-camped for a second time. This time, we taped the windows.

Everyone was pensive and subdued, but at least we were out of the city.

Bombing was distant now and as the day ended, we went to sleep. The following morning, I had a live by Zoom appearance on an Irish TV show, followed by a call to the national radio programme.

At about six the next day, missiles landed less than 2km away, destroying bridges and the roads. We heard the crump and saw the ball of light rise from the ground, followed by the sounds that uniquely identify what it is.

As I spoke on the radio show a couple of hours later, russian bombers flew low over the house and towards Irpin, where they were attacking, with bombs, missiles and paratroopers falling with their equipment from the sky. I stood looking out of the bedroom window as they raced past, so low that you could see every part of the plane and the dark outline of the sadistic murderer that piloted the warplane.

But, on the ground in PetrPavlBorshegovka, things were calm. Men patrolled the streets. The apple orchards and fields were empty, no immediate threat to be seen. I knew this could change, and scanned the skies, even though I knew others were doing this more consistently.

I had a call and messages from friends sheltering in places in Irpin, I knew what was happening to Hostomel, Bucha and

Irpin. Many russians, chechens and some belarussians were there. It was a time of hard battles and many of these invaders were soon dead.

I was sent a video by messenger from a friend. He was looking outside his window, over-looking the forests. Eight soldiers in russian uniform were gathering together around one who had a map and a handheld device.

They skirted the fence of his house, not looking around. It seemed these men were trying to get to a particular place and my friend's house wasn't it.

Some days later, darker events would take place at this and other places in Irpin, Bucha, Hostomel and Vorzel. Things that will live in infamy. Things I know, some that you also know.

Things that define terror.

At about eleven p.m., I had a call from my friend Oleg who lived in Irpin.

"Brendan, there are seven of us, we will make a run for it over country roads and try get away. Will you come with us?"

I knew I had left documents and money in Irpin. I needed those. But I had left money with Svetlana... maybe... No, it was too dangerous and Daryna too frail. Another disturbed night would do damage to her.

I agreed with Oleg that his group would pilot the route, sending me safe passage to Khmelnitsky, where Oleg had set up a safe house, at the edge of the city. He agreed to call at three thirty a.m. to see if my mind had changed. After that, they fled Irpin into the dark of an unknown night, driving across country fields, farm tracks and through tiny settlements, almost too small to be called villages.

A restless night followed, no news from Oleg, but I could

hear the battles in Irpin. Outside the house, neighbours took turns watching the night sky, armed and ready for any parachutes. We would be warned if danger approached.

It was after seven a.m. when Oleg called again. They were safe, but the route was difficult. In some places, russians were landing into the fields. He would send me the route section by section. Thank God for Facebook messenger.

We left at eight, saying goodbye to Svetlana's neighbours, most of whom were also leaving. A couple of the men stayed to protect the houses. I hoped all would be OK for them but knew that this area wasn't protected by Ukrainian armed forces. If the russians landed, they would be killed to prevent any alarm being sounded.

With everyone in the car, I went back into Svetlana's house. I took two long sharp knives and added them to the short one I already had. When I got into the car, I said to Sofia, "If I grab one of them, you grab two and give them to me as I need them." Sofia looked at me with alarm in her eyes. After a brief pause, she quietly said, "OK."

I was committed to defend my family and knew I would kill if I could. I had no doubts about that, not one. I am no big strong tough guy, but I would kill if we were threatened.

Travelling dirt roads, back roads and through housing estates. The first 100km took fourteen hours. By official roads, Khmelnitsky was 360km and usually took just over five hours. The unbroken lines of vehicles merging at farm crossings and dirt tracks meant it was going to be much, much longer.

At three p.m., I had agreed to speak to LMFM, my regional Irish radio station. In any case, we needed a break.

We stopped at a small village shop which was having its busiest day ever. Sofia and Aleksandra went to the shop, I took the call. It was the producer.

"Hello, Brendan, can you hear me?"

"Yes, very clear."

"OK, listen to the adverts and we will put you through to the studio. Just say what you want… no editorials, I promise."

"OK."

Previously, LMFM decided to have me and a local man living in russia on at the same time. This man was given the opportunity to speak fist and he was parroting the russia line. I was precise, calm and composed in my demolition of his comments. To be fair, he is one of many that simply and unthinkingly recite what they hear or read.

This time, it was different. The war was intense and the world's attention was focussed on what was happening.

As the LMFM presenter started, he introduced me and asked, "OK, now, Brendan, where are you?"

I explained what I had been doing in a matter of seconds and said we were just stopped for a break in a small village.

He then asked, "So what's happening? What can you see?"

As I started answering, the cat, Tosha, decided to make a break from the car and ran past me, shortly followed by Aleksandra and Sofia, running like Olympic athletes in pursuit of a cat seeking freedom. It took a flying tackle in the corner of a wooden church for Tosha to be caught, all while I was talking live on air. I nearly lost my concentration and had to walk away from the drama, along the narrowed country road filled with cars.

I saw Sofia had returned to the car with her prize possession, dirty and dishevelled, as was Aleksandra and the cat. But I maintained my concentration as I spoke to the radio host.

As I looked back to where we had come, I mean back to Kyiv, I saw something low, moving quickly in the air. Warplanes came overhead... russian ones. There were two, then another two. Moving at tremendous speed, making the whooshing sound as they passed... they banked and turned. They were circling back!

They screamed overhead as I was talking... "Warplanes, warplanes, got to go, got to go!" The radio presenter was cut dead.

I was in the car and trying to get out of the way. I drove calmly but the car was silent for some hours, everyone completely aware that we were in a real situation and being bombed from the air was a real possibility. The producer messaged me, and it was sometime later when I could assure them we were still OK. For now.

I understand this clip made the headline news on TV and radio, at six p.m., nine p.m. and later. News that we were OK was communicated later.

It was a week later when listeners learned my fate, as LMFM asked me to come on the programme again, but between times, all media wanted me and I was happy to WhatsApp message them, Zoom call them, and chronicle the events by sending videos.

On the programme, I first apologised scaring everyone half to death. My mother, God rest her soul, would have been furious. I can hear her now... "Brendan, don't be scaring people half to death... think!"

"Yes, mam! Sorry."

"So, you should be!"

After twenty minutes, we were out of the way of the

immediate threat as the warplanes disappeared in an unknown direction. These planes are low, very fast and come and go in a split second. It was clear. Our lives and journey could only be measured 1km at a time. There was no certainty of life, of the route and the destination.

Like the rest of the world, I was to learn later that escaping cars had been attacked on roads with people killed and injured. We were lucky, very, very lucky. I have sympathy for those less fortunate.

As traffic eased with more route choices emerging, Oleg was messaging changes in direction.

Avoid this road, change direction, attack taking place. The journey was phases and Oleg and his friends scanned information like professional military.

As we drove, we saw gatherings at bridges, junctions and crossroads. People with weapons gathering and waiting for vehicles for the journey to Kyiv, others working with tractors and large concrete blocks to create block posts.

Have your own opinions, but I saw a people rising, building defences of concrete and sandbags.

As we journeyed on, another message pinged.

"Brendan, this is Dave in Dublin. I have sorted out accommodation for the next leg to Ternopil. It's all arranged, I'll send details later."

Dave is an Irishman married to a Ukrainian. It was Dave who sought help with the campaign to make Ireland visa-free to Ukrainians, a month or so, before the war.

We arrived at the safehouse at about six, sirens wailing across the city. Welcomed with tea and food by Oleg and Wioletta, his fiancé. There was one bed for all of us, in one room, up steep wooden stairs. I was touched as this was for

141

Oleg and Wioletta, but they vacated it for us.

To make room for everyone, possessions and domestic appliances had been strewn across the first-floor landing. Little did I know that in a couple of weeks, my own possessions would experience turmoil when we reached home in Ireland.

There was a double bed and a mat on the floor, with blankets folded and at the ready when needed. Messy, yes, but nothing missing. The family that owned the house certainly did everything and I am very grateful for them for all they did.

Sofia, Aleksandra, Maria and Daryna took the bed, I slept on the floor under the window, next to the bed. Maria was closest to me and was wide awake, sticking her tongue out and making funny faces. We both laughed. The others, well, they instantly fell asleep.

Getting Daryna and Maria safely up and down had been a challenge, but one of the least demanding so far. Soon, we were all asleep, but not for long.

There were five families in the safehouse, and the clutter of possession was spread across every room. In the kitchen, there was food aplenty so when I went down, I was instantly offered coffee. A couple of minutes later, Sofia came down.

After we left, the number grew to eight. A couple of weeks later, they all lived underground in a concrete cellar under the house as sirens warned of cruise missile attacks on Khmelnitsky.

At around ten, we surfaced to find the car had a flat tyre.

Oleg, his friends and a couple of neighbours effected a temporary repair by inflating the tyre, then we drove to find a place that repaired tyres. There was a truck stop 5km away where there was a repair service. They agreed to fix the tyre, even though they usually only do trucks. They did it for

50UAH, about 1-euro 40cent.

As we waited, I prepared to speak on Irish national radio. It was Saturday, 26 February, two days after the attack.

Things were very serious now and this was the main national broadcaster. The producer said I had free reign, as usual broadcasting rules didn't apply, and I steadied myself. Immediately before being on, the stress and challenge inhabited my usual calm character and I started to lose composure.

It was an internal battle of wills not to cry, and I managed it, just, and not for long.

Live on air, I spoke strongly. Ireland was headquarters for many global corporations. "They need to close russia down," I said. "Ireland has been good for corporations with low tax rates and state assistance. Our workers are amongst the most productive in the world and they make billions.

"CLOSE IT DOWN, CLOSE RUSSIA DOWN!" I demanded.

"People of Ireland, help these corporations. Demand they close all their russia-related operations…"

Then I was in full flight. Powerful and demanding, I had the platform, and I said my piece. Thank you, RTE, you gave me an open platform and I said my piece.

I will be eternally grateful to all the journalists and producers, in TV, radio and the papers, who allowed me to speak unedited, uncontrolled and unhindered to the Irish people.

I will forever be grateful to the Irish people, across the Ireland, who listened, who took action and made change. And by God, was there big changes!

A whole system skittled in a matter of days. Restrictions

lifted and doors removed from their hinges. Thank you!

After the call, I cried uncontrollably and physically started to shake. Standing alone, distant from my friends and saviours, I looked across the empty fields, I only saw the grey sky and cold fields, the skeletons of trees that became dormant well before this infestation of evil struck. It was a cold, lonely moment, the countryside looking blankly at my distress.

At that moment, I realised that any future my family had would be in the hands of friends and strangers alike. We were on the run, from a terrible enemy. I had to be calm and do my job. 1km at a time.

Returning to the safe house, we had breakfast and reviewed the news. Attacks had occurred in Khmelnitsky, Ternopil and Lviv, but these were missile and bomb attacks. Troops and Tanks had not fallen from the sky.

By twelve, we began the journey to just outside of Ternopil and our Irish organised safe house.

A journey that would expose us to considerable danger and an encounter with soldiers in the dark of night.

Chapter 8
A Country Road to Ternopil. Soldiers, Battles and Risk of Death

The road to Ternopil from Khmelnitsky is 112km of well-built dual highway, which normally takes just under two hours. As we set off on a bright afternoon, I felt four hours should be enough, given the traffic.

Leaving Khmelnitsky, I drove past the tyre replace, following Google maps. After about thirty minutes, I realised we were going in the wrong direction and tried to turn round.

Like many modern roads, the dual carriageway had a hard separator of the lanes going opposite ways and it took another fifteen minutes to find an opportunity to turn round.

Ten minutes into the return, I could see in the distance a gathering of cars heading towards Khmelnitsky and I thought it strange that the road was very busy, because, when I had driven the other, these lanes were empty.

We soon caught up with the traffic and I noticed men on the road, redirecting cars to turn to the left, crossing the outbound road. Google Maps was going a little strange, but these men were clear so I followed suit.

The road was asphalted and single carriageway, typical of roads going through villages, it was clear we were going south of Khmelnitsky. A man stood on the road about 20km later and pointed right. He was armed with an automatic. There were two cars behind him, one a police car, the other a typical car, silver, something like a Chevrolet Saloon of some type.

Following a big black Mercedes, I turned onto a concrete road, like the one to Lazurne; *bump, bump, bump,* like a train. About an hour on this road and it turned to a cobbled road of considerable antiquity… the noise changed, and driving became much more uncomfortable. On one side of the road were fields and the other woodland. I had no clue where we were.

The road had huge potholes that needed careful navigation and after another hour, we continued, only the road was soil, compacted, no doubt, by farm machinery.

After another forty minutes or so, we headed through a stone wall, catching a stone as we dipped onto a field and we crossed, following what was clearly a track made by other cars, till we got to a farm gate with stone pillars. There were armed men there as well, with four vehicles, and they pointed to turn right, onto another asphalted road.

After about an hour on this road, we reached the dual carriageway and took the left, which we presumed was Ternopil, as the signs had been removed.

We stayed on this road and as I drove, I took a couple of calls from journalists. At certain points, we stopped and waited. After about fifteen minutes, Ukrainian armed forces passed us going the other way at speed. Big military trucks, military coaches and fuel trucks, followed by a white coach and a high-sided white truck.

As the troops passed, everyone cheered and beeped… so did I.

Off they went, while we stayed on the road. Once they had passed, we waited ten minutes then we were on our way. An hour and a half later, we were stopped again, and the reverse happened.

This happened twice.

Google Maps was behaving strangely. Suddenly, it would try to re-direct us off narrow country lanes to dead ends and it made no sense. As everyone stayed on the main road, I did the same.

After it had happened a third time, I realised that someone was interfering with the maps to block certain roads to restrict the movements of the Ukrainian military. It was the only plausible explanation, and I was glad I had not changed direction. It could have easily led to russian forces and trouble, if not death.

We were still far from Khmelnitsky, and it was dark. I had packed a 10l can of fuel and there had been nowhere to stop on our journey. Baby Car was in need of a refill and the girls needed a toilet break.

As traffic stopped again, I saw coming up a bus shelter with drive-in, designed so the buses were not blocking the road. I waited till we were near and pulled in.

Sofia and Aleksandra went off into the dark to go to the toilet, I opened the boot looking for the fuel can, which was hidden under the mass of bags and Maria's plastic toilet.

Taking things out carefully so there wasn't an avalanche onto the road, most especially laptops, I got the can and turned to face a very tall soldier with gun, in full armour. Behind him there were two more. I nearly died.

I didn't know if they were Ukrainian or russian, but these men had the physique of seasoned soldiers. The first man, being much taller and powerful than me, was in my face, hands on his automatic rifle. Oh ffff…

In the panic, I couldn't understand him at first and this caused problems… but then, I pointed to the fuel cap with the can, and he seemed to understand. I was speaking English in the stupid hope he would think it was OK… how mad!

The girls reappeared with two other soldiers, white-faced.

Documents, documents!

Jesus, where were they! As I fumbled for my ID and Ukrainian Residency Permit, the girls got the rest of the passports.

Sofia explained that we were from Kyiv going to a safehouse in Ternopil. It was dawning on me that these were Ukrainian forces and I relaxed. They were always calm and professional. It was only us that were in bits.

After checking the documents in the dark using a torch, the tall soldier returned my documents and calmy said, "OK… on your way." Oh my god… that was a surprise.

Getting into the car, we returned to the line of traffic and started to relax. The girls told us how the men had emerged as they were in the dark and scared them, but the soldiers had said it was OK. Laughing now was a way to de-stress.

It was only later we read about evacuees being shot dead by russian soldiers at stops like this. One chilling story relating to a man who was shot dead whilst relieving himself.

But that wasn't our fate.

As we passed a very large block post, I thought how big and heavily armed it was and was happy that I wasn't using a phone. Taking photos was forbidden and while the soldiers were calm and professional, it would not be a good idea to test them.

As we neared Ternopil, we went through three more block

posts, each bigger than the rest.

Our intended host, arranged by Dave in Ireland, was Mariana, who lived in a Ukrainian village outside of Ternopil called Velyki Hai. Sofia called her and she had bad news.

It was past nine p.m. and Martial law prohibited anyone leaving their homes; we had to stay in Ternopil overnight.

We tried to find somewhere to stay, but everything was in darkness. I mean everything. Other than the light from passing vehicles, all was in darkness.

After twenty minutes driving around, I returned to the main crossroads and followed a sign that said 'Hotel'.

Five mins later, we were in a dark car park of a modern hotel. Everything was in darkness and I wasn't sure if it was open. Sofia and Aleksandra went in and returned five minutes later. It was full and entry restricted. The man had locked the internal doors and was sitting in the dark.

He said that we could remain in the car park overnight, until curfew was over. That was seven a.m. He warned us that they recommended finding an underground car park to shelter from missiles.

Looking around the area, I could see no such car park and decided it was better to stay there. At least, he would allow us access toilets and recharge phones, which we did.

The long constant droning of the sirens was interrupted by Daryna's groans as she was very uncomfortable and in pain. Other people in cars were there also and next to us, in the back seat, was a woman breast-feeding an infant who could only have been a few days old. A split-second look was a portrait of distress on her face; her young, bearded husband looking on from the front driver's seat. A snapshot image burned into my memory, like a photo on my phone.

Twice, Sofia had to take Daryna out to stretch her legs, both times she was nearing collapse as her knees were swollen and sore. It was then, sometime around three a.m., looking at the stars blinking in the dark night, waiting for the sounds of cruise missiles that I thanked the Irish government for taking so long. We were five hours between Kyiv and my Irish home by plane. Five hours!

While Maria slept wrapped in coats and blankets, everyone else partially slept. I watched the vehicles and the Ukrainian troops rush past on the main road several times... and then it was 07.01. Time to go.

We were close to the village and off we went, right then left.

The long single carriage road had no cars, but soon we came to a block post, where they checked our documents and allowed us past. Shortly, we came to another. Sofia explained again and we were allowed through.

Getting to the house we were intended to stay at meant driving up a steep slope and along narrow roads, but at the highest point we turned onto a street ninety degrees to the hill and came to a stop.

The street was full of both old and new houses, well-kept and comfortable. Where we stopped was the place we were staying, and Sofia called Mariana again. To our surprise, we were told that others from Kyiv had arrived, and we needed to call Nadezhda.

After a conversation, we returned to the bottom road and waited. The sun was up and getting a little warmer, but still cold.

We waited and waited. It seemed a long time, but maybe only ten minutes had passed.

As everyone was getting impatient, two men walked up the road and motioned us to drive further. To a second place, where there was a small shop, which was closed, having a thick brown steel door firmly in place.

Opposite the shop was a large two-storey house in large gardens, behind black wrought iron fencing. As we drove towards the house, the men opened the double gates and motioned for us to drive in, which we did.

This spacious house was to be our safehouse from 27 February to 1 March. Daryna was in no fit shape for further travel and everyone, including me, was very tired. We had been in Baby Car for twenty hours.

When we got in, it was cold. The house had been empty for a while, and the men busied themselves getting the heating on. Aleksandra was anxious about the Internet, which was soon working.

Sofia and I took one large bedroom, Daryna another. Despite there being many other bedrooms, Aleksandra preferred to sleep in the living room, which was OK.

I had been asked by the national broadcaster RTE to create some video diaries and I used this time to produce one each day. It was useful for the journalists and even more messaged for photos and some comments. Three days after the start of war and I was hot news. It would last until I crossed the border with Poland, where I was met by RTE's senior correspondent Paul Cunningham and his cameraman, Owen.

The first one showed how tired I was... very, but over the following days, I managed to rest, as did everyone else.

We could 'shelter in place' for a couple of days, knowing that block posts protected every road. I felt safe and we could walk, eat properly and drink tea. There was even time for playing, laughing and generally being normal.

As we settled in, I got a message from an Irish LinkedIn connection who lived in Brussels.

'Brendan, I am thinking of you and your family. With that said what can I do that is more practical? As you know we are in Brussels and have space, I'm not sure what your plans are but if you are looking for a place to stay, we would welcome you.'

It was 4 March when I could respond, accepting the kindness of Yvonne and her husband Peter. Two truly kind, loving and considerate people.

I decided on the 28th that we needed to go. The growing migration crisis was building, and missiles were hitting cities, including Lviv. I had read about some conflict between African men and the train service Ukrsaliznytsia at Lviv train station, and reports suggested that waits at border crossings were over four days.

I told everyone that we needed to be closer to the border and we would leave in the morning. Not everyone was happy, but nothing was said, until the morning. At that time, I had a few offers of accommodation, but each took me further away from border, either south or north, than Lviv. In that moment, I was open-minded.

At 04.22 a.m. my phone pinged. It was from a connection request I had accepted just before going to sleep a few hours before. It was Luba. Someone I didn't know.

'Thank you for connecting. Do you have WhatsApp or Viber? Do you still need a place to stay?'

I answered.

'Hi yes please, I need to have options'

Luba then wrote.

'Can we talk?'

In two hours, I replied. Everyone was asleep and would be awake about seven a.m., allowing me to take a call.

At 08.16, Luba called.

Her mother lived between Lviv and the border in a small town called Mykhailivka. She was eighty three and wanted us to come to her.

In a split second, I agreed. We had our heading, thanks to a Ukrainian in Philadelphia who was reading my LinkedIn posts. *Phew!*

It was after breakfast when I left the table to pack. Sofia was in the bedroom and had her bags all done. I heard a commotion and Daryna crying out loudly.

As I went through the rooms to the dining room, Aleksandra was shouting loudly, Daryna was sitting at the table and Maria was crying. Sofia was on top of Aleksandra on the sofa, which was used as a bed.

I immediately tried to get Sofia off, realising that Aleksandra had her teeth sunk into her arm at the elbow. I pushed between Sofia and Aleksandra and tried to get Sofia off.

Aleksandra was wild. She was saying she would kill Sofia and I had to pin her down to stop that happening.

"STOP, STOP, STOP!" I yelled.

"No! I will kill her!" Aleksandra shouted.

I eased my grip and Aleksandra lunged forward towards Sofia, as both Daryna and Maria cried loudly.

I pinned Aleksandra down and told her I would keep her there till she stopped. No matter how hard she struggled, I was too powerful for her, and it was a few minutes of stalemate.

I told Aleksandra to calm down and I would let her go.

She said OK and I stood up.

Standing now, Aleksandra lunged for Sofia again and I body checked her, pushing her to the wall, between the TV and the window.

Again, I held her arms and she screamed, very loudly and emphatically, "I WILL KILL HER… I WILL KILL HER."

Clearly, this was not going well.

After scuffles and struggles, Aleksandra started crying and relaxed. I let go and she fell into a foetal position on the floor. I told Sofia and Daryna to wait in the car, Sofia went to take Maria but Aleksandra shouted again and I said, "Leave her."

Aleksandra and Maria's things had been scattered and the TV had had a narrow escape, but tightly curled on the floor, Aleksandra's crying was useful.

I gave her time… Maria stood and looked, shocked and fixed to the spot.

"I WANT TO STAY HERE… I DON'T WANT TO LEAVE!" Aleksandra said.

"You can't. There are others needing the house," I lied.

It was true we needed to move because of the threats, but we could have stayed longer. My view was that things could only worsen and we needed to be closer to the border, just in case.

"I DON'T KNOW WHAT TO DO! I DON'T KNOW WHAT TO DO!" Aleksandra shouted.

I waited for a few moments and said, "OK, look, come with me to Lviv and you can decide there."

"NO! I WILL NOT GO WITH DARYNA AND SOFIA, THEY WILL KILL ME!" Aleksandra said.

Quietly, I said, "No, they won't, sit with me and I will look after you. Just till Lviv."

"NO, I WILL BE WITH MARIA!"

"OK, that's OK… you be with Maria as you have been all the time."

I left Aleksandra and Maria and went to the car.

"Say nothing," I said to Sofia. "Tell Daryna, say nothing… total silence."

"OK," they replied.

I went back into the house to see Aleksandra packing. Maria was crying, but the passions were subsiding. I had achieved something at least.

When everyone was in the car, all packed in as before, with Tosha in a cat carrier and Lisa under Daryna's feet, everything was silent.

I sat in the driver's seat and sighed. I then drove the car out, stopping to close the gates and take a picture.

I thought to myself, *You don't have much time, Brendan; things are very unstable.* As I looked at Sofia, I saw the marks of a perfect set of teeth in her arm, deep red but not bleeding. She said nothing. Good!

When we returned the keys to Nadezhda, she asked why we were leaving. Sofia simply said, "We had to."

We had 130km to go to Lviv and who knew how long that would take. All I knew was that it would be in total silence, bar the occasional cry from Tosha the cat, calls from Irish journalists and from my new-found saviour, Luba.

The day before we left, which was a Sunday, I had seen a curious post on Facebook that soon made it to LinkedIn alleging racism in Lviv train station, supported by a picture of African men looking very aggrieved.

I was surprised because racism isn't common and

155

certainly not in public transport, although some had manipulated a few incidents into BS stories, often emanating from pro-russian sources.

As I said, the car was silent as we drove.

The block posts were much bigger and complex now, the people there were formed of three groups; police, military and the territorial defence. All three were in bullet proof vests and had automatic and semi-automatic weapons. As we approached Lviv, heavier guns emplacements were visible, which made sense as the government had moved some functions here and this is where the US and other embassies had moved.

In my mind, I was thinking of post-war Vienna, full of people, intrigue and spies. It wasn't.

The main routes into Lviv were closed and we had to take a circuitous route behind large apartment blocks and small streets. Block posts at every junction, each one looking at documents and asking the same questions.

As we came into Lviv centre, I drove toward the train station reaching the edge of the large open space.

Cars and people were swarming, and I saw a parking spot open up outside a pharmacy. I slipped in fast as I could.

Silence.

Aleksandra was still silently raging, and her expression was as buttoned up as a coat.

I told everyone I wanted to go to the train station, which was about 2km away. I was happy to go with someone or go alone.

Silence.

Sofia and I got out of the car. Nothing moved in the back.

I had my answer. Sullen as it was.

Walking through the traffic, I could see police and security directing the vehicles and quickly going to anyone who had stopped. Clearly, they were afraid of some attack, and no one was left alone to do their thing.

Sofia and I crossed towards the large expansive space in front of the station, and I could see the crowds milling about.

Crossing the tramlines and walking towards the station entrance, I could see the tented village on the left and the bus station on the right. Ahead were few cars, but a mass of people.

As we approached, groups of men were exiting the front and walking towards the tents, outside of which were barrels with fire, food stalls and obvious signs of aid.

We went into the large hall and looked at the large, digital timetables high on the wall. Platform 1 to Poland.

We went to the platform and saw guides in fluorescent yellow jackets. A long line of women and children ahead of them.

Being a man, I was approached by one of these women; a volunteer, helping out.

Sorry, women and children only.

I stopped... *Ahhhhhhh,* now I understood. It wasn't racism, these African men had been denied passage and when they forced themselves onto the train (as in their photo), they had been challenged and removed, by the women passengers as well as the staff, to make room for other women and children, of all nationalities.

I stood taking in the atmosphere with Sofia, who was still not speaking much.

There were trains to Poland and trains to Kyiv, as well as local and regional ones. That was clear.

As we exited the train station, we went to the bus stop to

see about buses.

Women and children only was the first thing the driver said to me. *Of course.*

There were many in the line, with bags and baggage. Some so many that he refused them.

$100 a person, the driver said. *What?* I thought, *That's high.* But then, it was to Warsaw in wartime, with long delays at the border. Maybe he was right, I don't know.

Having gathered the information, I returned to Baby Car with Sofia.

Daryna had decided to wander off, looking for something to eat and buy.

I saw her leave the car and ran to catch up. The last thing I wanted was a missing person. She refused my invitation to return to the car, so I went with her, helping her to buy some food and a drink.

Sofia had stayed out of the car and as we approached, she sat in the passenger seat.

All aboard, I turned to Aleksandra and explained her options. Warsaw, Kyiv or come with us.

She demanded that she wanted to stay in Lviv. She had read people were offering free accommodation.

"OK," I said, "go, find someone, look for somewhere. You are free to do as you wish, I don't keep you."

Fiercely, she sat in her seat saying nothing. I waited.

It was her decision to make and not mine. Whatever she decided had to be her decision after the fight, if it was to be put behind us.

I had something to eat, and some water.

After five minutes, I said, "OK, I am going to drive."

"Where will we go?" Sofia asked.

"Mykhailivka," I replied.

"Where?"

"I don't know, but between Lviv and the border. It gives us options as to which border crossing depending on the situation."

"Oh, OK," Sofia said. "Let's go."

"Right, can you get it on Google Maps?"

"Yes."

I turned to Aleksandra. She looked straight ahead, not looking at me. After thirty seconds, I started the engine and once Google Maps came up, started to drive. All hands on board.

Chapter 9
Mykhailivka

It is a little over 77km from Lviv to Mykhailivka and 48km to the border. Normally, it would be about two hours from Lviv to where we were going and an hour and half to the border, but reports had said that the journey was completely blocked with traffic and that the border crossing could take four days, if not more.

Anyway, we were as close to safety as possible.

We had left Lviv the way we had come, and it was clear the block posts were getting much bigger and complex. Longer with a number of chambers and headed towards Rava-Rus'ka, which is the last town until the crossing Polish border at Hrebenne.

Luba is a great person, chatty, friendly and warm. As I drove from Lviv, she called again, to check on progress. Luba is also innocently honest, and she spoke about her mam, Nadya. Nadya is eighty three and very active, she said, going to describe a force of nature that was at once kind, fearless and also a little lonely after her husband had passed.

"Brendan," Luba said, "Nadya has been trying to help people and has been disappointed. Some people came from Kyiv but decided not to stay, as the house is old. Maybe you will think the same and if so, just say and leave, it's OK."

Odd! I thought it odd but dismissed it. I was unlikely to

say no. Luba also said, "By the way, I told my mam that if you weren't nice, she should kick you out also."

I laughed, then looked into the rear-view mirror. *Hmmm. Oh crap!* I thought as I drove the road to Rava.

It was a cold but bright day, and the traffic was light, which was not expected. I half thought we would have a hard time of it, but no.

We stopped at Rava for water and for Daryna to buy some food and we travelled onward. The road was pretty open and flat, nice, and I was beginning to feel a little bit removed from war. Until, that is, when we came upon another block post, and country lanes leading to small settlements, farmsteads really, entirely blocked by concrete and manned by armed locals.

We were waived through and about 6km later, entered Mykhailivka, which is a evenly spread-out town of low-rise buildings, both historically interesting and modern.

A clean town with wide streets, Nadya had asked to meet us in the centre, which to be honest is just a maze of narrow streets, with a market and a few shops.

When we got there, we were supposed to follow a road up a gentle incline and find a church, so I drove where I thought was right. Up ahead on a high ridge was a very large statue of a Pysanky egg, brightly painted.

I was happy we were going in the right direction until a junction forced us left and then right, conveniently returning us back to the road where the church was.

A call to Nadya was made and she speedily spoke about directions, she was in town shopping and would be there soon.

With our new directions we headed back to the church and started again, heading towards the pysanky egg, which was almost beacon-like.

"Turn right at the church…" *Yup, there's no shortages of churches in Mykhailivka, and this one was the most anonymous-looking church you can find.* "Past the health centre and school, then head on up, see the house with the big green substation on the corner, that's my house…" Got it!

Not really.

The road bent to the right and at the corner there was a left-hand turn. We were soon returned back to the first church. *Groundhog Day!* I thought.

Driving in total silence can be a blessing or a curse. I could feel the tension and annoyance, but no utterances were made. Thank God! Well, not for the church, but for the silence.

I tried again.

As I approached the same bend, a tiny woman in a hat and long coat was speedily walking, at the speed of an Olympian runner, up the road, which was going uphill. The woman had a bag in one hand and a phone to her ear in the other. My phone rang. Nadya!

I stopped the car, but she waived me up the road, so I drove ahead, upwards along a narrow road lined with well-maintained large houses with gardens, similar to those you find in many Irish villages and towns.

The car-lined street with hedges and fences were very familiar and as I drove, Sofia said, "Look, a green substation," at the same time as I said the same. *Snap!*

At the side of the substation was a large set of metal gates, behind which was a tall, imposing redbrick house at the bend in the road.

Our Olympian host was with us the moment I stopped the car, composed, not breathless, despite the steepness of the hill and the distance. *Wow,* I thought, *what a dynamo,* and tiny.

Maybe less than five feet with dark hair under her beret.

Nadya soon had the metal gates open and ushered us in to a large garden, with a greenhouse to the left and a white brick shed ahead of us. To the right was a three-storey house, the ground floor being rendered in grey cement.

As we got out and exchanged hellos, I marvelled at where we were. In the walls of the ground floor were double doors to what was undoubtedly a garage and ahead of us were steep, wide and tiled stairs leading to the entrance to the house. I also noticed a single door a metre from the double garage doors, above which were large windows, two for the first floor and one for the third.

My oh my! It was great.

The steps to the main door had three landings, turning to ninety degrees. Tiled in pink sand-coloured ceramic tiles, we all followed Nadya, who was trying to open wooden double doors, varnished in clear varnish to showcase the wood. The doors had window panels built in, with black wrought iron.

Nadya opened the doors to reveal a second set of doors and inside was a large spacious hall with two exits, one to a large bathroom, the other to the hallway that led to the inside rooms.

The title of my book is a dead giveaway that I am Irish. I was born, reared and will die Irish. It is my blood, my family and my character. The only odd thing is my accent, which soaks up others like a sponge, meaning it's not colloquial... Sorry, neighbour, I can't help it!

Part of my growing up, if you remember, is going to the convent, for summer garden parties and for Midnight Mass at Christmas.

Standing in the hall, I was transported all those years back to the Convent entrances' own hall… wow! This was a mighty fine house with high ceilings and a settle calm atmosphere only too familiar.

We were ushered through white-painted double doors into the hall and to the left.

The warmth that greeted us was sleep-inducing. Like a cloud, the warmth of the wood fire in a plastered brick fire embraced us as Nadya spoke at a million miles an hour. I had no clue what she was saying, she was too quick for me. I soon found out she was too quick for everyone else also.

The fire was, in fact, an oven, with build-in cavities for cooking and an open top, with metal plates for pans. I loved it… I really like such things.

This room had double doors on opposite walls. One led to a store, which had a ladder made of robust steel pipes leading to a roof. The other to a large bedroom, where Nadya slept in winter.

On the opposite side of the hall closest to the exit was a comfortable bedroom painted with a large rainbow. Luba's old room, on the left was a really big and very grand dining toom.

Within seconds, Aleksandra, who was still not speaking, took Luba's room. Daryna snapped up the room with the oven.

Within seconds of opening his travel cage, Tosha the cat ran to the room with the latter and up to the top. There he stayed. Lisa, of course, was bolted to Daryna's side.

Nadya pointed to me and Sofia. "I have a great place for you!" And she ushered outside and back down the stairs into the garden.

When she got to the single dark brown painted wooden door at the foot of the stairs, she jiggled some keys and opened it.

We followed.

Bloody Hell!

Two years ago, we had stayed in a magical place called Chudodievo which is a village restaurant complex 10km down a narrow-wooded track. Very modern and well-planned, Chudodievo was built around a large lake and wetland, at the edge of a beautiful forest.

The wooden houses were both single and like chalets.

We had stayed in a chalet which faced into the woodland gardens, under which there were play areas and small buildings, one a small conference hall, another an underground store, another a really well-designed restaurant, whose interior design was elegant and chic.

The windows of the restaurant looked through the forest to the lake.

As part of the deal, we had four hours in a sauna house, which had been built next to the lake.

Windowless, save for a couple of small, opaque ventilation windows, the door of the sauna led to a wooden hall and into a living room, with dining area, sauna and plunge pool. Of course, there were toilets and a shower.

It felt like an underground hideaway, and we enjoyed it each time we visited.

Nadya's hideaway was just a fabulous and extended under the whole of the house.

The first room was a kitchen dining area which was warmed from a wood fire. Well equipped, the smells of cooking filled the air.

To the right-hand side was a large storage room that was mostly empty and directly behind it was a living room, bedroom, with table, TV and all the creature comforts. This was to be our home for the next few days.

As we all moved our things into our respective rooms, it seemed the mood was lightening and Nadya was talking with everyone, who happily answered. Being smart, she soon picked up the vibes and understood that perhaps Aleksandra and Maria would eat separately to us.

Before I knew it, Nadya had Aleksandra and Maria eating in the large dining room and Daryna warming herself on the bed near the room with the oven. Sofia and I were happy to 'move in' and get settled, charging phones, laptops and the like.

Nadya loves plants and everywhere inside there were pot plants, looking their usual untidy selves as it was 1 March. Outside, of course, everything was in hibernation, but large patches of ground had already been dug to overwinter properly.

As Aleksandra and Maria ate upstairs, Sofia and I had tea in our underground den, as Nadya cooked and chatted with us. This was lovely.

The smells of chicken stew filled the air.

Soon, Nadya ushed us to the dining room, recently vacated by Aleksandra and Maria who were in their chosen room, door firmly closed.

Immediately on entering the dining room, I was asked to open some red wine, bowls of very tasty stew was accompanied by cold meats, sausages, a beetroot salad, bread, biscuits and tea. Very tasty and enjoyable. Nadya's irrepressible, good mood was infectious, and the vibes softened, people even smiled, laughed and were animated.

This was perfect, in that it could change the dynamic and possibly instigate some re-engagement.

Later, Aleksandra was going to walk back into town, and I agreed to take her. Few words were said, which was right. Given the sensitivities, words matter, and the last thing I needed was offense to be taken over a misspoken comment.

As the evening drew in and the chill of a freezing night descended, people were quiet, tensions subsiding and emotions calming down.

The underground bunker Sofia and I stayed in was an added shelter from harm. Isolated but not remote, we had time for ourselves in the self-contained rooms. We were warm and in a lighter mood.

The morning saw a hard frost on the ground and my thoughts went to the many in cars, hiding in the forests and fields at the side of the road. We had passed many on our night-time drives and I had sympathy for them.

Cars can be near instantly cold when the engines stop. Fuel stations were few and far in-between, so keeping engines on was not going to happen.

I did see cars broken down, some looking for fuel. Often in remote places, but others were always stopped and offering help. In this journey, people were not being left alone.

Other vehicles stopped for a break and as passengers clustered together, expressions were the same. Blank, unsmiling and bemused. Most were standing apart, eating or drinking. No one was laughing or being enthusiastic. People were stoic and that's all.

Baby Car ran light, but many cars were big gas guzzlers. While I would have had times of anxiety when the fuel light flashed on, the next fuel station with fuel being an unknown, I am sure the drivers of bigger cars were stretched and anxious much more often than me.

At one place, I turned across the road, not realising there was a long line of traffic. A pump attendant came over and politely pointed to the line, indicating my mistake. I drove to the end and waited... forty-five minutes. Everyone was quiet, respectful and patient. No panic. The prices were not much different than Kyiv and no one was price gouging, despite the temptations.

Refuelling had been a calm and disciplined experience for us. The limit was 20l, that's all. Some of the owners of gas guzzlers had many ten- or twenty-litre cans in the back and I remember watching one man haggle with the pump attendant, as I waited behind him.

I watched as he gestured and offered money in an underhand kind of a way, but the attendant simply pointed to the cashier. Off the man went, in expensive designer clothes and a certain confident stride. His wife and children had gone on ahead and returned to the car before him, coffees, drinks and food in hand. A car picnic was clearly in store for them.

He returned to the pump and the attendant pointed to the car and then the cans. He had put one out and there were four more in the open back of the SUV. It was obvious a choice was to be made. The man pointed to the car. Once he had gone, with all his wealth and certainty, parking further up so they could eat, I drove Baby Car into the space left.

As I looked at the pump, I smiled... 20l... He got the same as everyone else. Not more, not less. No drama... he got 20l.

I got the same.

As usual, I was up early and a made my video report for RTE. Reflections on the day. I have never seen them since, and never looked for them online, but I knew from messages from

168

reporters wanting to speak with me that they provoked interest.

I am recognised by strangers in Ireland now, they smile and say hello in a familiar way. It's nice. They do so for Daryna, Sofia and Aleksandra also, which is great.

After filming, I had a call from a journalist who was coming to Poland and wanted to catch up when I crossed. No problem.

As I walked the steeply sloping garden answering his questions, I lived in another world, from war, in a neat and well-kept garden thinking about my next move, while speaking to someone whose copy would be read across Ireland.

It's only afterwards you think of consequences. But words matter, opinions matter, people matter.

Soon the ground will warm and Nadya's famous flowers will bloom, and she will travel the three hours to Lviv to sell them in the market where she has had a stall for many years, walking the 3km to the station only to do the reverse on her way back.

But now, it was frozen solid.

Nadya was her usual dynamo self, preparing a wonderful breakfast for everyone and we all stirred. 2 March was here, and we had a day of rest as I thought about our next move.

We were as safe as possible in Ukraine and I felt comfortable in staying to see what was going to happen, but I also knew that planning ahead was necessary.

More offers from within Ukraine came in for us to stay, and then a friend, Mykola, re-connected me with someone based in Poland. I had spoken with them before about consultancy work, but this was a kind humanitarian offer. I got another later that day from someone else in Poland; each offer being a little away from the main road I would need to take for Ireland.

Sofia then told me that her brother Yura was in Poland. In Warsaw, and he offered accommodation. So, we had options. 'Always have options, Brendan,' my father would say.

My father died when he was ninety two and he did so with an intact brain and a devilish sense of humour. Intelligent and worldly wise, he credited fighting in WWII with his own and his generation's emancipation from the treadmill of options that were in prospect.

He was an engineer in the war, fixing tanks. He fought from North Africa, Sardinia, Italy and on to Austria, supporting the front tank regiments. A sergeant major at twenty one, he was matter-of-fact about killing and death, impressing on me the need to be well-informed and diligent.

He was in live combat but was never sure he killed anyone, but he would say that he sure did try.

He described organising his teams of men taking busted tanks and putting them back into service. He described brushing out body parts, pairing ears, legs and arms, sorting out dog tags, for the others to take way. He didn't see it as morbid.

He spoke passionately about the fighting Poles, who won Monte Casino, where he also fought. He spoke about opening the Vienna opera for the first time, proudly showing me the opera guide and the special thank you note with his name in for making it possible.

He introduced me to his work colleagues who had been garrotters, snipers and men of war.

He despised the occupation of Ireland and what British soldiers did there. He once coldly told me about a 6'4 young man who told him to his face that he was going to kill Irish people in Belfast. He lasted only a few days, returning to his English home at 4' something… without legs.

My dad's stories were important to me as I searched for clues on what to do best. It was my mother's voice that spoke loudest. 'Do your best and let them go. They will find their path.'

Everyone was keen to hear my next step, but I wanted to do it separately.

I told Aleksandra we would decide what to do, but likely we would go to Ireland. I told Sofia the same.

I made it clear to Aleksandra that if she wanted, she could go to Lviv. It wasn't a problem.

I told Sofia that Daryna needed to be brought to safety.

During the day, I was getting messages from Irpin. Hard war. russian, chechen and belarussian troops, massive bombing. Kyiv under severe pressure, Chernihiv also. The enemy was at the gates and Irpin had said, "NO! YOU SHALL NOT PASS."

Photos of dead people, killed in the street, burials next to the railway line, at the side of car parks and in the sand of the playground.

The hardest to hit home was the mother and son (just a small boy) shot and buried in the green edge of the path next to the road, on the corner of the street. That and photos of bodies wearing coats I recognised. People I would see in the local shop, sitting in the park with their children, or chatting on the benches.

It wasn't safe to evacuate just yet and all bridges were destroyed. That could have been us.

What was unknown at the time was revealed later. The

rapes, torture, murder and wanton destruction.

By May, the atrocities were known about all over the world, and the Human Rights Commissioner reported rapes from two to seventy eight years old. But we were in March, six days after the attack.

That could have been us.

I don't know Yura.

Sofia has a very large extended family, due to her father's multiple marriages, I do know her father worked hard to connect the children and often would bring them together. Yura came to our wedding with his wife and children, bringing another brother, Mark.

He seemed a decent guy.

It was Yura that opened the door to Poland as he was in Warsaw with his girlfriend. They had moved there and were based in the city centre. I wasn't involved in any of the conversations, but he had good relations with Aleksandra, and he had good relations with Sofia, from past gatherings and shared times.

Cruise missile attacks on Khmelnitsky and Lviv pushed my thoughts to crossing the border.

Later that day, Nadya asked me to go to the town centre with her. I happily obliged, thinking that she wanted to buy some food. When we got there, it was clear she was a woman on a mission.

She asked me to stop the car and went into a Piva store… A shop specialising in beer. Ignoring the barriers, she got some beer and went to pay.

"Sorry, it's not allowed," said the young girl at the till.

The human dynamo raised herself to full height and asked, "WHY?"

"Martial law. No alcohol anywhere. We can't sell it."

I knew this as I saw people in Irpin online, breaking bottles at a shop that had ignored the law. Later, they would empty the alcohol out and use the bottles as Shevchenko Smoothies, as Molotov Cocktails had been re-named, but at the time, they were throwing bottles of wine, beer, Champagne, cognac and other drinks against a wall to break the glass.

Not to be denied, Nadya asked me to drive to another shop where her friend worked.

Thing about eighty three-year-olds who worked hard, cared and contributed to community is that they have a status which is difficult to deny. When we entered the shop, Nadya spoke to the owner who waited till everyone had left the store.

Five minutes later, she opened the locked glass cases and waived me forward. "Choose your beer, Brendan," Nadya said. I looked and chose. Lvivska.

Putting the bottles in Nadya's big black leather bag, the owner locked the case and walked away. No money required. As we left, she smiled at me and wished me good luck on my journey to Ireland.

"Thanks," I said.

We enjoyed the beer with dinner. This time, all of us being together, even taking group photos.

The following day, it had snowed. I filmed my video reports and we had breakfast, before saying goodbye to Nadya.

Before I left, Luba called and demanded that I don't leave anything behind. No money, nothing, it had been a pleasure. I agreed, but lied.

We left the breakfast table, which was the dining table, and took more photos. As we packed the car, Nadya stood outside.

I quickly returned and put $100 under a plate. Not much,

173

I know, but my money was very limited, and we were far from home.

Taking a last few photos, me with Nadya on our own, we left at 08.45 and headed for the border. All aboard!

Chapter 10
The Border Crossing

Leaving Mykhailivka meant going the way we came. As we drove through the town, I wasn't sure of the traffic but when I looked, I saw the border crossing times were only a few hours. It was cold as it had snowed, but it was bright and sunny.

Paul Cunningham from RTE had messaged me when we arrived to Mykhailivka, and we had kept in touch. I had my documents from the Irish government, which was essentially a 'safe passage' letter. We had no passport for the cat nor the dog, and Daryna's passport was ancient. My passport was in my home, that had been bombed, not that I knew it yet. We were going to Hrebenne.

I trusted that all would be well but understood that the next hours would be defining. Inside the car, the mood was light, but conversations minimal.

The traffic out of Mykhailivka was heavy and I couldn't understand why, until I got to the block post guarding the town. It was massive. Checks were serious, polite and efficient.

Then we had an open road till we joined the Lviv to Hrebenne road.

Then the road was open, and we drove at speed, reaching the T junction and turning right in good time.

In ordinary times, the distance of 19km would take no time, but now, well who knows.

When we reached the main road, it was absolutely clear and open. The sun was bright, and I was happy to be moving fast, although the blue sentry box-like portable toilets regularly set out indicated that the Ukraine authorities had worked to address previous issues with standing vehicles.

As we approached the checkpoint, signs made it clear: NO CAMERAS.

The open road slowed a little as coaches and minibuses parked on the right. Lines of people meant we stopped. I watched the solemn and sad scenes as people said goodbye. Ukrainian men were not allowed to leave Ukraine, so they said their goodbyes.

Some of their wives chose to stay with them and teenagers waved tearfully as they walked to the border, some with young children and babies in their arms.

One boy, maybe eight years old, walked alone, his backpack almost as big as him, toy in hand, as his parents waved.

My heart was stilled at the scene. It was a scene like no other… moments that lasted lifetimes seared into my memory. Stoicism, bravery, courage…sacrifice. Heart-breaking. I wanted to cry, but now was not the time. I sighed and drove forward into the gap emerging between us and the car ahead.

We got to the Ukrainian side of the checkpoint at 11.20 and I messaged Paul. *'Great, not long now then,'* he said. If only he were a prophet! He isn't.

The first gate was customs. A quick look in the car and we were good to go to the next point.

At the second point, still on the Ukrainian side.

"Documents."

I handed them all and waited. About fifteen minutes later,

we were waved to the next part… The cordon.

But that was OK. It was around one thirty p.m. and I thought, *Cool, this is going well.*

Next to the Polish side.

"Documents."

We waited and waited.

"You need a green card for the car," said one of the guards, "pull over."

15.06. Sofia was escorted to an office block, and we waited an hour or so for her to return. We were not allowed out of the car, so we sat, watching the world go by. It was 16.06 when she returned, clutching some white A4 papers.

The guard waved us on to the barrier 20m ahead.

"Documents."

We waited and waited. Paul and his cameraman messaging me, patiently waiting.

Immigration. OK.

Next, customs.

The guys in customs just wanted the car documents and I thought it would be five minutes. Nope.

We waited and waited as the bright skies darkened into the darkness of the night.

The guards had taken the documents into an office which had a window that slid open. I saw a hand waving.

I got out of the car and walked forward to see my documents hanging precariously on the shelf. I took ours and went back to Baby Car.

As I walked, I realised I had the documents of the transit van behind us as well, so I walked back. They wouldn't let me give them to the driver, so I returned them to the shelf.

It was 17.45 when the barrier lifted. In the dark, I drove

out towards a melee of parked cars at each side of the road and an encampment to the right. As I drove, I saw Paul and Owen, stopping as they filmed.

I was heartily welcomed by Paul and Owen, and we went straight into the interview, the car door open and me half standing on the road, one leg inside the car. It was great to be with them. Finally, Irish people!

In the yellow glow of streetlights, Sofia, Aleksandra, Daryna and Maria stayed in the car as I did the interview. Then they sprung out of the car and headed to the encampment leaving Daryna and the animals in the car… Toilets! Of course.

Not thirty seconds passed when a policewoman and man came over. "Sorry, you can't park here, you have to drive round," pointing up the long dual carriageway.

Unthinking, I jumped into Baby Car and drove. Daryna started screaming, sure that I was abducting her and abandoning the others. Despite my assurances, she was yelling blue murder.

The road went far before any possibility of a turn, and I worried about getting lost. The phones didn't work now as we were outside of Ukraine.

I turned down a single-track road that had a small arrow pointing to the camp and drove, trying not to speed as Daryna unleashed her fury.

Arriving on the other side of the barrier and embankment where I met Paul and Owen, I saw the three of them, shopping furiously.

Maria was covered in a blue blanket, given to her by care workers and there were covered market stalls with food, drinks, clothes, hygiene supplies.

Stepping out of the car, Daryna, in her dark brown fake

fur coat released her final rebuke and staggered to a picnic table where Sofia had assembled refreshments. By 18.07, she was sitting in a white plastic chair, which glowed yellow under the lights, drinking hot coffee with a cherry pastry, her dog Lisa by her side. Being the villain I am, she ignored me entirely… *phew!*

The stalls and hot food were greatly received, but the melee of people, being brought by car, coach and minibus was sobering, but we needed to go.

Warsaw was ahead.

Three and a half hours later, I pulled into a motorway service station to be met with signs directing us to a part of the car park behind the buildings. 'Ukrainian Refugees This Way'. The arrow being suitably coloured blue and yellow to represent the Ukrainian flag.

A much bigger reception centre was laid out, more food, refreshments and clothes were on offer. All free. McDonalds was open for toilets, and I used it for Wi-Fi. Something we did repeatedly on our way through the EU.

As I went for something to eat, a realisation dawned on me as I spoke to a volunteer. I was a refugee. We all were.

That realisation is a challenging one. Something I am not keen to repeat. Watching others getting out of their cars, out of buses, coaches and vans, I saw the same expression of bewilderment and confusion. This wasn't supposed to happen. This was entirely wrong. What had we become?

An hour later, we headed to Warsaw city centre and Yura. We arrived after two and I parked in a multi-storey.

We all slept peacefully that night, me in a corner on cushions, like a dog. The others shared a big pull-out dark brown sofa. Tosha in his carry case and Lisa gripped firmly by

179

Daryna.

The next morning, we went to walk around the city. Svetlana, Sofia's sister from another mother messaged offering us accommodation in Hannover, but first we needed to rest and get some sim cards.

To get some air, I went to explore Warsaw with Aleksandra, Maria and Sofia.

A city of wide streets, big buildings, both old and new, and busy shopping districts, Warsaw is modern and assured.

We were impressed by the Ukraine flags and posters in solidarity with Ukraine, most especially the huge banner style flags which brightened the monolith that is the Palace of Culture and Science, whose dominating presence in the centre of the city made for a useful reference point, as it was close to where we were staying and easily seen from any vantage point that we had.

Nearby is a modern glass shopping centre and we ventured in, somewhat dazzled by the busyness, colour and vibrancy after our journey of isolation, small places and even smaller shops. It was a teeming metropolis, something we hadn't seen since we were in Kyiv. Was it only eight days ago?

Some days before we had left, Sofia asked that we go to a newly opened shopping centre called Retroville. This large and stylish mall was about twenty-five minutes from Obolon, and we had visited twice before. It struck me as odd that as we wandered around this complex in Warsaw, Retroville was in ruins, after being bombed and completely destroyed by russians days before.

Here, saw many Ukrainians doing what we were doing, which was figuring out sim cards and money. Hryvnia, the Ukrainian currency, being difficult to exchange at a reasonable value. When we returned, I messaged Yvonne, hoping that the offer of accommodation in Brussels was still open. It was.

It was 4 March and I also needed safe passage to Ireland. I emailed Stena to set out our situation at 16.47.

We needed a ferry from Cherbourg to Rosslare. Two minutes later, I was included in a referral email and shortly after had a call from Sylvie.

Sylvie was absolutely perfect, asking me to send details necessary for the ferry. To my surprise it would be free, and Sylvie would not only book everything, but would liaise with both customs and immigration in France and Ireland.

By 17.19, all documents and details were emailed to me. Thirty-five minutes and all done. Thank you, Stena!

We bought pizza and rested for a second night, me being the dog for a second time, sleeping in the corner on the floor.

We left for Hannover at nine, once Daryna had walked Lisa in an urban park. The photo is reminiscent of one taken of Rudolph Hess in his later years whilst incarcerated. Why that popped into my mind, I don't know.

On paper, Hannover is 823km from Warsaw, passing Berlin. Normally, it would take between 7–8 hours, if we didn't stop.

It was obvious that passing Berlin would be a crime against Sofia and Aleksandra. Having been there before, it was easy to suggest we add some time to the journey, most especially as our accommodation would not be available until after ten thirty when the facility, a non-residential day care facility for elderly people, closed.

181

Chapter 11
Germany

From Warsaw to Berlin is 572km and should take five hours thirty-eight minutes according to Google Maps.

In Poland, dual carriageways were fast and free. As soon as we reached a toll, the registration plate reader would open the barrier and we would pass through, slowing down as we passed through the narrow control points. But hey! No documents... welcome to Europe!

Once we went to Germany, things were different, the most significant being the sim cards we specifically bought to work all the way to France stopped working. We had to stop and buy replacements. Tolls were also paid, as I had euro, unlike Zloty, so I was OK.

Until I realised how many tolls there are... Wow, pay, pay, pay...

Germany is well respected for its great roads and experience bears out the reputation. Good, fast and without any hassles. But it is a big country, and it took six hours to get there from Warsaw. Largely because of traffic entering the city passed Schoenefeld (Brandenburg) Airport.

Having visited Berlin before, I drove through the city to Alexanderplatz, driving slowly so everyone could take in the views on the first pass. Getting to Alexanderplatz, I turned round and parked.

All packed in, as we had been since leaving Kyiv, I opened up the opportunities to visit as Sofia and Aleksandra googled places to see. Aleksandra wanted to see a church and Sofia just wanted to look round. All were on this road. Daryna was happy to look out the window.

Returning from where we came, I stopped at the Berliner Dom, a cathedral that was typically Germanic, gothic and heavily designed.

"Thirty mins," I said as I parked the car.

Sofia, Aleksandra and Maria jumped out as I rested and Daryna silently gazed at the strange world around her. She was in Berlin. Never had she imagined that she would be in Berlin. Not ever.

In front of the cathedral is a park, adjacent to Lustgarten, where many people walked, and behind it, in the distance, I could see a street market. Lost in my own thoughts, time passed.

An hour and a half later, I could see Aleksandra taking photos with Sofia and Maria, each one staged, even the ones where they were jumping, the camera on timer. Obviously, Aleksandra wasn't happy with the earlier ones, and they tried multiple times.

I thought, *Good… they are having fun. Very good.*

Like Warsaw, there were many signs of solidarity with Ukraine. The blue and yellow banners flying lazily in the breeze. *Time to breathe a little,* I thought. Time passed and I could hear Daryna become restless and beginning to mutter complaints about the wait, which I ignored.

In time they returned, not realising how long they had been and happy. Always good.

I decided to drive slowly down Unter Den Linden to the

Brandenburg Gate.

As we drove down, Sofia and the others saw the many sights I have seen, as well as many others. Passing the large russian embassy, which is opposite the Reichstag building, we could see a large police presence and security bollards to prevent any encroachment.

Our little blue Skoda Fabia 1.2, packed with bags, people, a dog and a cat slowly ventured down to the small pedestrian space around the Brandenburg Gate.

"Stop, I want a photo," Aleksandra cried.

"OK, two mins, there's no parking here."

"OK."

Tucking into the side of the road, just past Madame Tussaud's Waxworks Museum and a car dealers, I stopped, engine running. Sofia and Aleksandra jumped out and ran to the solid-looking stone arches.

Inevitably, it developed as a photoshoot as I anxiously looked for trouble. Just behind Baby Car was a police station with a police car outside. From the door of the building out stepped a policeman.

Mindful that I was in a packed Ukrainian-registered car, almost opposite the russian embassy, in a strict no-parking zone, I expected trouble.

The policeman stopped, looked around and saw Baby Car. As Sofia and Aleksandra danced about taking pictures, he started to walk towards the car. *Hmmmm, going to be trouble.* As the sim cards didn't work, I couldn't call them; in any case, the phones were on the seat. They had left them and taken Aleksandra's camera. If I was forced to drive off, it was a long way till I could stop and who knows how I could find them if we were separated.

Thinking to sound the horn, I hesitated, this guy was armed, and anything stupid could escalate the situation. I breathed, trying not to call out to the girls who were too far away to hear anyway. *Sit still,* I thought to myself. *Just sit still. Breathe... This is so not cool!* I thought.

Behind me, Daryna gazed out the window, taking in the scenes and Maria slept. Crap!

As the policeman came close, he stopped, looking at the reg plate, blank expression on his face. A Ukrainian car. I could see his expression change when he realised. There were many clues to where we were from, to be fair.

He saw me looking in the mirror at him and he waved, hesitated and walked the opposite direction and crossed the road to be on the side where the russian embassy is situated. Nothing to see!

Phew!

Five minutes later, the girls returned to the car in flying form, laughing and joking. I was determined to stay silent and not undermine the mood.

Taking the right-hand side and driving around the Brandenburg Gate, we had the opportunity to see the Reichstag properly, stopping for a short while but not getting out of the car. I drove up Street des 17th Juni passed Ronald Reagan's (of Mr Gorbachev, take down that wall! fame) monument and through the Tiergarten to the golden Victory Tower.

As I drove, it struck me as ironic and awful that we were fleeing the extension of World War II, through the future state of what was a destroyed Berlin, understanding that corruption and appeasement rendered all the great words and noble sentiments on this road were trashed. Totally and utterly trashed.

While the images and truth from Irpin, Bucha and Hostomel wasn't known to the world at that stage, I had seen some images taken by neighbours and friends. As I drove, I was sombre. It wasn't only Irpin in ruins, it was the promise extolled by the monuments of these streets.

Not only my neighbours were dead, so too were the international security agreements, treaties and laws that made this street peaceful and the adjacent fields and wooded parkland places where families could play, relax and be free.

This street and what it stands for, is dead. Only few knew it then, perhaps only me.

Reaching the ring road again, I turned and headed for Hannover.

It was around six p.m. when we entered the on-ramp for the road to Hannover. 286km to go and three hours thirty minutes in terms of time. As I settled into my usual driving mode, I relaxed. Everyone was chilled and satisfied. Except Daryna, who thought the waiting for Sofia and Aleksandra an imposition. Despite being repeatedly told we had to wait till ten thirty p.m. to have access to the accommodation, she was insistent it was an offence to leave her in the car.

Arriving into Hannover, we stopped in a McDonalds for refreshments.

Parking at the back of the restaurant, we parked and everyone got out.

Aleksandra and Maria headed for the toilets while Sofia walked slowly with the shuffling Daryna, who was, to be fair, struggling with the journey.

Food and drink bought, Wi-Fi accessed, we sat at different tables.

Letting time pass, I dawdled. No point rushing to stand still, we had time.

As we ate our food, Daryna having a hot dog and coffee, buying a second hot dog for her dog, Lisa, we checked our social media. However, the back and forth between Aleksandra and Daryna didn't abate. By the time we returned to the car, tensions were high.

Google Maps showed us the road and we were at the appointed location exactly at ten thirty. Looking for the address proved unsuccessful, as the apartment-lined street proved somewhat anonymous. We found the number of the house, but not the address. It was strange.

As Sofia and I walked separately, looking for signs, trouble was brewing in the car... to boiling point.

Sofia called her sister Svetlana and at just past eleven thirty p.m., she arrived. Taller, with silver blonde hair, Svetlana was relaxed, active and well-organised. Her dog, jumping out of her car, keen to make friends.

They hadn't seen each other for twenty years, so it was a surprise re-connection. Svetlana was much older than Sofia and from their father's first marriage. Long since living outside of Ukraine, it was providence that she was in Hannover and had access to some space.

We were staying in a respite centre for elderly people, Svetlana was the manager.

By day, the rehab rooms would be filled with old people undergoing treatment, while the very large TV rooms would allow those waiting to be distracted. Two large kitchens were testament to the size of the numbers of people being treated, as well as the numbers of staff.

As we all brought in our bags, Svetlana showed us the treatment rooms, each one with a hospital bed. As it was

Sunday, 6 March, the centre was empty.

It was clear that we would have several clinical rooms and that the staff kitchen would give us a place to eat. The showers and toilets were good. Just one thing.

We needed to be gone by seven, before the staff came to work.

All bags in, Aleksandra was in open revolt; she would not stay with Daryna. NO way.

Noisily demanding something else, Svetlana defused the rage by inviting Aleksandra to stay with her, leaving us to stow away our bags.

After some tea and some chocolates Svetlana had gifted us, we went to sleep. Sofia, Tosha and I in one room, Daryna and Lisa in another. Sleeping on medical beds, which were impressively comfortable.

We slept soundly and as usual, I was awake first. Not long after, Sofia and Daryna were up and we had breakfast. I asked Daryna to forget the previous day and say nothing.

About an hour later, before our time of departure, Svetlana returned Aleksandra and Maria who had also breakfasted, and we left, grateful for the kindness of Svetlana, who was almost a stranger.

It was the 7 March and time to head west again; this time, to Brussels, and the true kindness of strangers; this time, Irish ones.

It was five and a half hours to Brussels, some 483km, I could only hope peace would be sustained, but for me, I was happy... Irish people, I would be with Irish people... finally! But for now, it's pay, pay, pay all the way, even for public toilets!

Strange people.

Chapter 12
Brussels

I love Brussels, but shudder at the historic abuses that one can see once you get past the facades. I especially love Brussels as the centre of a social and economic experiment of collaboration and cooperation, the European Union.

It was our lovely Irish family that had offered their home to rest, and I greatly appreciated their kindness. The kindness of strangers and a testament to the good in people.

The ferry was in three days' time, and they were happy to accommodate us for that time. For me, I wanted to settle everyone and defuse tensions.

It isn't easy to accept strangers, especially into the privacy of your own home, particularly when you have children. It can be stressful. I have found it so in the past and would experience it again, once home in Ireland, but that's for later.

When people are experiencing emergency evacuation, it can be additionally difficult, as behaviours may not be within accepted norms. When this happens inside the sanctity of a home, it is very sensitive.

So, let me say with all my sincerity, this family brought us into their hearts and home openly and with warmth, most especially their young daughter, the eldest of two and clearly boss of the house, who, when we arrived, gave Maria a present and took her by the hand, leading Maria into a world of toys and imagination that brought the child back from where it had been hiding for eleven days.

From the first moment of our arrival, Maria had been in the capable hands of her new 'big sister' who, in reality, was only eighteen months older, but a wise, intelligent and loving person, all the same.

Hand in hand they walked the house, ran, played with a shop-sized array of toys that took up a large part of a very large room, went upstairs and talked... the talk of children whose shared language isn't the same words, but child speak.

By bedtime, Maria was fully inducted into the sisterhood, and I was very happy to see it.

I have a photo of Maria from the day after we arrived, on 7 March, sliding down the green slide in the adventure that was the back garden, smiling as she had done last in Kyiv.

So, to this Irish family, thank you for restoring the child in Maria. The three-year-old was back.

Something similar happened to Daryna, in that she was adopted by one of the two large dogs of the house, who would follow her and sit under her legs, being her guide and protector in this wonderful Irish family home.

Fortunately, the family had a superb TV system, and it was possible to access Daryna's favourite programme and for the first time outside of Ukraine she could relax in a familiar way, sitting on a large comfortable grey sofa full of cushions, watching TV while this big dog sat under her feet.

Lisa, Daryna's dog, seemed somewhat slighted, but stoically sat nearby, although it has to be said that Lisa was instantly befriended by the dogs in the house, in a similar manner to the girls adopting Maria. Each dog wandering round with a cool attitude, indifferent to the world of humans.

That there was no jealousy or difficulty is a tribute to our hosts, whose warmth, genuine sincerity and love permeated the walls. Their cleaner, who we met on the first morning, also had the same warmth and for me, well, I was impressed. Truly a wonderful family.

The house they have is a large three-storey house on a quiet hillside housing estate of modern houses, close to a park. We arrived having navigated the intricacies of narrow streets that seemed to be an impossible-to-understand maze of tidy residential streets, where houses and small shops and pharmacies cohabited easily.

Once arrived, we were warmly greeted as long-lost family, and nothing could have been kinder. Separate rooms, great food and Belgian beer... superb!

Their home was in a really nice area close to a landscaped park, and it was good to walk and talk, with our host, instead of the feeling of being 'on the road again'. As we talked the usual banalities of life and living, I could feel the normality like a warm embrace. The area is steeply undulating, giving the feel of space and depth, despite there being many houses, which, in this 3D landscape created a community feel rather than an urban expanse.

I really admired the architecture of the houses, which were low-rise, individual and stylish. Despite no two being identical with many differences, the whole environment came together as a whole.

The park, only recently re-opened after covid restrictions, was clean, airy and comfortable, with sloping pathways, cycleways criss-crossing undulating parkland, with trees and lakes. Urban nature at its best.

Later that day, I had suggested that Sofia, Aleksandra and

I go to the city centre the following day, our host was happy to mind Maria, while Daryna simply needed to rest and have some medicine.

The following morning, we awoke, perfectly rested, and everyone in a good mood. The sun was shining, and it was far from cold. The host's children were in kindergarten and so I played with Maria in the back garden, where swings, slides and other children's furniture added to the many things of interest in a sloping garden with mature trees, which were home to squirrels that Maria found fascinating.

It was here I took some photographs of a happy, confident and comfortable three-year-old, little realising that the horrors being played out in Irpin, Bucha and Hostomel included the rape, torture and death of children of her age. That we would find out on 14 March, as the defeated russians were replaced by Ukraine forces and the international media.

We had planned to go into Brussels that afternoon, by bus, but beforehand we needed medicines.

Daryna has been stressed over her medicine since leaving Kyiv, and Sofia and I decided to go to a nearby pharmacy to get something. Voltaren or similar and something for water retention on her knees, so that Daryna could soothe her aching body after so many days on the road. At this stage, from the 14 February to 6 March, it had been eleven days.

As we walked down the steps from the first-floor main door to the street, I appreciated the sunshine and the absence of cold. It was a nice day. I knew the route to the pharmacy and was looking forward to the fresh air.

Heading down to the pharmacy, Aleksandra called for us to wait, she wanted to come with us. Happy to see this, we three went the ten minutes' walk to get the medicines and then returned.

We returned to a very unhappy host. Aleksandra had left Maria upstairs and hadn't let our host know and when she returned from being on the ground floor, found Maria wandering alone. This was highly unsatisfactory, and I was appalled. How could that happen?

After a short exchange, I was bereft... so sad and feeling guilty that we had caused an upset, but even more concerned about the disconnect in care. Our host needed to get her children and we ended with her saying we should go, but I hesitated, waiting till she returned to close the issue. Despite the passage of time, I still deeply regret what happened and while I prefer to think of it as an oversight on Aleksandra's part and poor communication by me that we were only going to the pharmacy, I do wonder why we fail so simply, but with such unintended offense.

Once I restated my apology, I left, taking Sofia and Aleksandra in the car. Satisfied that I had made my point by actions rather than argument and protest. I drove back to the main road that led to the city centre.

I had been warned by our host about the traffic, but I wanted to see the commission buildings. I had been there several times and enjoyed some of the panels many years previously.

I was invited to an environmental panel and was seated next to the Irish delegation. The British were sustaining their non-EU positions on environmental regulation at the time (well, before Brexit) and the hostility was evident.

I was connected with the translators who were, at least privately with me, irreverent, most especially about one south-eastern MEP who loved his own voice, droning on about matters that were not for consideration.

As I drove past the Schuman building and into the centre, I noticed military officers standing outside a building, each one in full uniform, sporting ribbons in the colours of the Ukrainian flag.

I was later to find out that these were senior military undergoing training at the EU Armed Forced building. The eight men were from Lithuania, Estonia, Poland and somewhere else. Two colleagues had been representing Ukraine but had returned because of the war.

The ribbons were in solidarity and a brave decision in that it was a political statement while in uniform. These were major generals being trained to become Lieutenant Generals, so very senior.

With all the turmoil, I didn't realise that my phone battery was low and as we entered the city centre proper, started to look for a phone shop.

I had been told that some quarters near the centre were dangerous, which surprised me. When I had been in Brussels, the quarters with large populations of non-nationals were very welcoming and cool. But, over the decades that had passed, the cordiality had, allegedly, been lost.

I stopped by a phone shop, dead centre of an area like this, if the people around me were any indicator. When I went into the shop, the man could not have been kinder and Baby Car's Ukrainian registration was cause for supportive comments from him and others who came in. These people were warm and friendly. Exiting the shop with a very discounted power bank and cable (which was free) I felt a bit better and drove in a wide circle to get back to the street that lead to the famous and historic Grand Place.

Parking on the ground floor of a multi-storey, I was surprised how quiet it was.

We walked down a quiet metropolitan street, following the signs. Everything was closed and there were very few people. Traffic was almost gone. Only on reflection did I realise this was very strange in a capital city, but it is a hallmark of the pandemic which we had not experienced in Kyiv, or Irpin, as the authorities had adopted a managed 'business as usual' approach, for most of the time, lockdowns being targeted and shorter than in Belgium.

Wandering the narrow roads, descending from where we parked, we turned to follow the directions. The street of well-restored buildings presented closed shop facades, as the darkness of an early March night rapidly drew in.

Entering the Grand Place from Rue des Chapelliers, the fabulous edifices of the baroque buildings towered majestically above us in the dark, light by lights strategically placed to highlight the architectural excellence, fancy and fun, each statue and carving telling a story from three hundred and thirty years ago.

Hard to imagine, but this incredible square was almost completely destroyed by the French and was rebuilt. It was rebuilt again in the nineteenth century, so not original, original, but a clear example of 'build back better'.

On this dark evening, the weather was dry and not too cold. There were very few people in the square, less than forty, and none of the tourism-related activities were open. Most of the shops were closed.

As I mentioned before, I didn't realise how strong the lockdowns had been and other than Starbucks, a couple of pubs, shops and restaurants, most were closed.

As we wandered round the square, I decided that a coffee break was required for all of us, so we could enjoy the scene from inside. I chose Starbucks because the large windows with seats let you do just that, whilst warm and being refreshed with coffee, or in Sofia's case, chocolate mocha latte.

Much to the delight of Sofia and Aleksandra, some of the chocolatiers were open and like 'Roshen' a superb chocolatier in Ukraine, they worked hard to create living retail spaces that were part fantasy and part hard sell businesses.

As we walked around relaxed, Sofia was offered a sample chocolate by the shop manager who was clearly bored and ready for home. We were the only ones in the shop and it felt like we were the only ones to have been there in a while.

It was, of course, a very reckless move, like an unknowing tourist putting their finger in the river Amazon. Sofia was and is a piranha for chocolate and her discipline dissolved at the opportunity to sample famed Belgian chocolate.

Sofia is very discerning when it comes to chocolate, like a sommelier is for wine. Not boring, but has a forensic approach to taste, what's in the chocolate, how sweet, bitter, flavourings…any hope that the manager had of an early home time evaporated.

I moved away and smiled. I could visit many shops and return later, knowing that Sofia would be deep into the complexities of chocolate… *Hahahahahaha!* I was free!

Twenty-five minutes later, I returned to rescue the manager and Sofia bought her conciliatory chocolate, as compensation for the grilling. Aleksandra hadn't engaged in the inquisition either but had remained in the vault of chocolate-like shop.

Our host messaged me asking if we were OK and letting

me know Daryna and Maria were happy. I was touched by the message and grateful that a dark cloud had passed.

We returned about nine thirty p.m. and enjoyed comfortable discussions about this and that, including what we had seen in the city centre. I also agreed we would go back into the city centre the next day, the 8th; this time by bus, taking Maria with us. To my surprise, it seemed that businesses had only opened a few days prior, explaining the quietness.

The morning was bright and even warm in the sun. We walked to the bus stop as directed and very quickly, fifteen minutes maybe, we were in the centre of Brussels. This time, it was before lunchtime and more shops etc. had opened. We had time and good mood.

Phew!

Wandering the famous streets, which were still relatively light in tourists, almost empty, but some at least. In fact, the biggest number of people was at a protest over women's bodies and rights, presumably because there were legislative changes being planned, but I don't know. All I know is that there was a gathering of about two hundred, predominantly women protesters, near the bust centre, chanting, singing and blowing whistles.

We walked extensively, including the Parc de Bruxelles, St Michael and St Gudula Cathedral, and the Jardin botanique de Bruxelles… a good walk and a truly touristy day.

We saw many Ukrainian flags fluttering gently on the church steeples and the roofs of high buildings. There were many posters. I wanted this to be a total holiday, going sightseeing and leaving other things to one side, which we did. The show of solidarity was encouraging and well-received.

Walking every street, or so it seemed, we saw many tourist

sights and enjoyed the famous chocolate, waffles and tasty beer. We took countless photos and Maria marvelled, along with us, at the sights.

Sofia was bemused by the Manneken Pis but having witnessed so many enjoying the fun of it, came to see it a little more positively. "It's fun," I said. The response to which was a withering look of disdain.

After a long enough day, we went back by bus, getting off a few stops earlier so that we could look at the small shops that nestled between the houses in Brussels' clean and well-ordered streets.

The next day was 9 March and the ferry in Cherbourg awaited us at nine p.m.

Before we left, we went shopping for some small tokens of appreciation and some Belgian beer; Aleksandra being a big fan of it.

Our farewell was as good as it could be, I had restocked their beer, but Sofia and Aleksandra had 'borrowed' a couple of bottles more, without my knowledge. We gifted small presents and some wine. I felt entirely inadequate and socially awkward, but Baby Car was fully loaded and off we went... Next stop, Cherbourg and the ferry. Pleas from Sofia and Aleksandra for going into Paris had been muted by our host explaining about the traffic, delays and impossibility of parking.

Thank you, I thought.

And with that, we left... grateful again for the kindness of strangers.

Chapter 13
Cherbourg and the Ferry

All packed, we said our goodbyes and drove to a hypermarket as Aleksandra wanted to buy some beer. Sofia wanted to buy some things too.

Despite the wisdom of our hosts, Aleksandra became increasingly disappointed at not going to Paris, especially as we passed the signs for the Paris Road and continued towards Cherbourg. The brooding in the car was palpable.

Our hosts suggested a quick visit to Caen as a possibility and no one objected.

Pay, pay, pay through the toll roads was our regular experience until we got to Caen.

We stopped near the Abbey of Sainte-Trinité and parked.

Sofia and Aleksandra went off to take photographs while Maria slept and Daryna gazed blankly at this historic town, about which she had no knowledge.

Checking out documents so I had them to hand, I was enjoying a warm sunny afternoon, hoping that the next step, perhaps the most important since Rava – Hrebenne, would go well.

Sylvie had assured me all was in order, and I had no reason to think otherwise.

What could possibly go wrong? I asked myself... You will see.

Arriving at Cherbourg ferry terminal is a strange experience; the road is long, and you are unable to turn or change direction for a long way. Consequently, when you take a wrong turn, you have a loooooong way to go.

Arriving in good time, I was happy and turned right... a mistake. It took about twenty-five tense minutes to get to the junction again, turning left and down another long road to the first checkpoint.

"Documents, please!"

I gave the documents and started to explain. The young guard had some English, calling to his superior in French. He then went off to show the documents and process them.

Ten minutes later, he came back.

"Mr Murphy, where is your passport?"

"It is in Irpin."

"Where?"

"A place called Irpin, we were the first to be bombed..."

"Oh OK, but why did you leave your passport?"

"I didn't want to be killed."

"Yes, I see... OK."

Off he went to tell his boss my answer.

He came back with all his colleagues who gathered round the car and wished us well. A gesture of humanity that was unexpected but welcome.

Now to the next checkpoint. Stena Line.

"Documents, please!"

"Where is your passport?"

"In Irpin!"

"Where?"

And so it went... then... "Where are the pet passports?"

"OK, listen, Sylvie in the office has the details, it should be on the system…"

"Oh, OK, wait, I will call her."

"Mr Murphy, Mr Murphy… Sylvie has left for the evening, and we have no records."

"What!"

"Sorry, but we don't have everything…"

As the representative was explaining to me the issues, her phone rang. It was Sylvie returning the call.

After a conversation in French, the young woman smiled. "OK, Mr Murphy, Sylvie explained everything, and you are good to go. Here are your documents and a tag for the car, hang it from your rear-view mirror and join the line. All is OK. The pets have places as well, please ask at reception and they will take you where you need to go.

"Enjoy your trip and I wish you and your family all the best. Good luck in Ireland!"

"Thanks," I replied.

Phew!

We moved up behind a motorhome and waited… the line of vehicles blinking red from their lights.

Soon we were waved on and ascended the ramp into the cavernous ship. Following instructions to turn and park.

As we alighted from Baby Car, we were directed to a green metal door that was open. Leaving everything, but taking the pets, we went to the lift and ascended to the third floor.

"Ukrainians to this side!" said a woman and we joined the line.

We were greeted by the staff and given all our electronic vouchers, being guided to our room.

First, we were taken to the place where the cat and dog would stay and got them settled. They were the first, but as they were quartered several dogs arrived. The crew member making pains to given them water.

Sofia and Daryna were assured that they could visit anytime, which they did.

The room was warm with three sets of bunk beds. More than enough room, but so warm. I opened the ceiling vent and we left Maria and Daryna to get our bags.

When we returned, it was cooler but still warm. I felt the rumble of the engines and we all realised we were off. Goodbye, mainland Europe!

We decided to get refreshments and I went for the vouchers. Card in hand, we went and chose food and drinks. For the first time, my Ukrainian family tasted fish and chips, with salt and vinegar, bread and butter... they were in love!

Refreshed, we went to sleep in the much cooler cabin. We all slept well, the vibrations of the ship being constant and reassuring.

After breakfast, the day became sunny with clear blue skies. With the open sea as a backdrop, we took photos, laughed and enjoyed the sea air.

We were due in Rosslare, County Wexford, at two thirty p.m. so we had loads of time to unwind, which we did.

We also had vouchers for lunch and much to my amusement, everyone chose fish and chips again... twice on two days! Scandal! I laughed. They were happy to eat and relax.

I was excited at the prospect of land... important land... IRELAND! My home, my soul and my people. The only place where I truly belong, spiritually, other than in Ukraine.

After lunch, I was very keen to tell everyone I could see Ireland, but they were too busy with chatting and taking photos, but as time progressed, the small dot of land emerged larger, greener and fully defined.

Announcements had us gathered and ready and as everyone returned to their cars, we went for Tosha and Lisa, our cat and dog.

By the time we got to Baby Car, many vehicles had already left.

We soon got to the vast openness of Rosslare ferry terminal, and we were called over by a woman in a fluorescent jacket.

Bubbly, warm and speaking in a wonderful Irish accent, she wanted to know about the pets. Writing down the details and responses to our questions, she asked me to sign and told me they needed to be kept at home for two weeks. No problem!

Then she waved us on and we joined other Ukrainian cars, parking behind the Motorhome once again, and waited. And waited. And waited!

After two hours, we went to see what was what, and a man came out and said, "Another hour, lads, is that OK!"

He wasn't asking, so we went back to the car. In any case, the room was full of Ukrainians so there was nowhere to be, but the car. Standing outside at a cold ferry port terminal isn't for me.

An hour and twenty minutes later, Sofia and I went inside. "Documents!"

As we started to introduce ourselves, one of the guys asked, "Who is that walking in the secure area?"

I looked out. It was Daryna... Having got bored, she wanted to escape the car and had decided to stretch her legs after sitting so many hours, waiting. Dressed in her signature yellow track suit, which she had worn every day till Brussels and put straight back on once our kind host had washed and dried them, she was easily recognisable on the windy open expanse of the ferry terminal exit ramps.

Sofia was dispatched to get her, Aleksandra and Maria.

"I know you!" one of the guys said, pointing to me. "You're the fella on the telly, radio and in the paper, the one who wanted to change the law for Ukrainians. I know your face, you did good."

"I am and thanks."

The others looked at me, looked at him, then looked at me... Some completely blankly.

He then started to explain about the campaign I fronted before russia attacked, but was cut off.

"Oh yeah, he is," said another. "I thought I recognised ye!"

Smiling broadly, the ice and formality well and truly broken. Now we could have a decent conversation about what this was all about. And we did!

The three guards (Irish Police – An Garda Síochàna) had been sent to process Ukrainians and had invited a Ukrainian from Dnipro to translate, which he did. But these were the first arrivals, and they were ill-prepared.

The Ukrainian translator explained that the delay had been caused by the first group arriving. The Irish were all prepared, until they learned that the group were deaf and dumb... No one was ready for that, so by sign language and Google Translate, they haltingly and slowly gathered the information.

When it came to us, the stress levels were relaxing, but Daryna's passport was a mystery. Having never left Ukraine, it was ancient, red and a legacy from the Soviet.

The translator told them it was a relic, to which, one of the lads replied, "All I want is a photocopy, anything else is for others to worry about."

As I was recognised and was Irish, they guards felt comfortable in asking questions, so we talked for an extra thirty mins.

I told them they would need a large marquee to the side of the cabin, and they laughed at the very idea, saying their bosses would never agree. Two weeks later, I was sent a photo of the reception, with large white marquee, exactly as I predicted.

In an anti-climax, we were given a document and the senior garda said, "Welcome to Ireland, to everyone..."

Cool! I was home, well, almost.

Another three hours and I drove up the single car track that leads to my house, crossing a small river by way of a bridge. Once at the bridge, it was my land. In the darkness, I could see my house, dark and silent, as it had been for two years. I also saw the overgrown yard and bushes. Nature was reclaiming the land... I would need to sort that out.

Opening the porch door, I put the lights on outside. All good, they worked!

With trepidation over what I would find, fearful of burglary or worse, I opened the door to my home and switched the next light on and we all went inside.

Chapter 14
Home

As I switched the light to the living room on, I was holding my breath. It took a second or so for my eyes to communicate the image and for my brain to register. I had been away for two years; would everything be the same?

No.

The first clue was a dead starling on the floor. Then another and another. Dead, dried out and portents of damage.

These birds had come down the chimney, which is a hazard in country areas. I can imagine the squawks and noise as they crashed around the house in a cloud of black soot, which they triggered as they came down.

Ornaments were broken and a film of black soot dust was everywhere. I mean everywhere.

As everyone started to gather, I collected up the dead bodies and hid them. Taking a brush to make a way into the house for the others, I was conscious of the mess and worked feverishly, but was never going to beat the tide of people, a cat and dog spilling into the house.

It was cold… very cold.

I put the heaters on in the bedrooms, which had thankfully been spared the dust, until, that is, when we brought it with us.

Kettle on, it became clear that the water pump wasn't working so I went to investigate it. Seized solid. That would have to wait.

I battled the dirt as everyone tidied to stay warm, everyone other than Maria and Daryna who, wide-eyed, wandered the house entering every room to see what their new home would be like.

Pretty soon, bedrooms were commandeered, but it fell into step with my thinking and no arguments. A single room with shower and toilet for Daryna, a double bedroom with toilet facing it for Aleksandra and Maria. My separate bedroom, upstairs living room for me and Sofia.

While everyone went to bed, Sofia and I cleaned, and cleaned, and cleaned. Then cleaned some more.

The next day was Sunday, and I was awake early… yup, cleaning.

We had bought some supplies for breakfast and then the chaos started.

My house has been my home for twenty-five years. Originally, a small stone single-storey house some three hundred years or so ago, it had been added onto over time, first two bedrooms, then a single-storey extension at the back to create a large kitchen and bathroom.

After my divorce, I added a living room and dining room to the ground floor, a bedroom and living room on the second floor to the right of the house and two bedrooms, one en-suite at the back.

A house of many rooms.

I went to the pump and started it… Nope, it didn't budge. I tried several times, then disconnected it, which is always a water sport that I dislike. Soaked, having failed to release parts of the pump. After fifteen years, they get sticky and I didn't have the right tools. I put it in the boot of the car and went to get changed into dry clothes.

Dripping wet, I couldn't strip in the porch like I could when I lived alone, so I soggily slopped into the house.

It was mad. Aleksandra was rootling through the kitchen cabinets and throwing things out. Sofia was washing the shelves before returning items. Looking at the scene, I decided that it was therapeutic so decided to let it play out.

I gave them bin bags so I could go through the rejected items later, like a hoarder, not ready to let go.

Dried and in dry clothes, I invited Sofia to come to Dundalk with me as she looked stressed and somewhat dominated by the manic cleaning being done.

Going down to the petrol station in Omeath, a small seaside village directly below my house, on Carlingford Lough's water's edge, I was met by the owner.

He wordlessly came round the till area and gave me a hug.

"Welcome home!" he quietly said.

He asked about the journey and how we were, took a selfie to send to his wife, who didn't believe it was me, and when I filled up, declined payment. It was at that moment that I looked up and down the village street and across the water to Warrenpoint, the mountains of Mourne standing behind them.

Looking up at the Cooley mountains, I whispered to myself, "Welcome home, Brendan... you're here now."

I have known Peter Durnin of Durnin Pumps since he started his business, and I went to his shop. As we arrived, it was clear he had moved. Standing outside the door looking for clues as to where he went, a taxi car pulled up, driven by a man from Dublin, according to his accent.

"He's gone!"

"Yes, I can see that," I replied. "Do you know where he

went?"

"Yeah, he's on the Coes Road."

Coes Road is a narrow road running parallel to Dundalk, and bisected by the inner ring road, forming two parts. It has many businesses along its length, and you need to drive in and out of small units to find a particular business.

Having tried for about thirty-five minutes to find him, I went to an electrical wholesaler than knows me at least eighteen years and I asked them.

They recognised me and directed me to Peter's new place, which was on the second part of the Coes Road, just past the engineering fabrication factory my neighbour in Omeath owns.

Tall, slim, short black hair with glasses, Peter came to the counter. A new premises, much larger than before, it was obvious that this dedicated, hardworking man was in demand. The premises were well laid out and very tidy, but due to covid, the counter had sheets of clear Perspex, to keep the staff separated from the unclean customer.

As he emerged from a workshop at the back of the premises, he came forward, his expression of recognition developing as he approached, just like a polaroid picture.

His welcome was simple and exactly typical from people from my community.

"Well!"

Yes, that's all we say… sometimes, the inflection is surprise, is questioning, friendly. Sometimes, it's a bit robust, but it is authentically my community. Unarguable, understated and enough.

"You made it then," Peter said after I replied.

"Yeah, I made it."

"Good. I was following you on the radio and the television. You did OK. Is your family with you?"

It was only the second time to speak about this and as I spoke, the words were unfamiliar. Years travelling gave me a non-local voice and I have a weakness; in that, I pick up accents wherever I go. Peter was struggling following what I was saying, but he got the theme of things.

After a few minutes, he said, "So... what can I do for you?"

I asked him to follow me to the car, where Sofia was sitting patiently.

Opening the boot, Peter said, "So you came all the way in this wee car?"

"I did..."

"I see," he replied in our typically understated way.

As he looked inside the boot, he saw the mess that was the pump. Fourteen years ago, he had sold me this to replace another in equally terrible condition, warning me that I would lose the syphon if I wasn't careful and that I needed an in-well pump.

"Ahh," he uttered. "So?"

As I told him, I pulled the pump out and we went inside his place.

"Brendan, you didn't dismantle everything, you should have done this, and this, and this..." I accepted his criticism. Peter loves his work and is very conscientious. I was a man under pressure and did what I could with inadequate tools.

Testing the pump confirmed what we could see... totally seized.

Peter set to work to try and free up the pump, while asking me about our journey.

After ten minutes, he conceded defeat.

Finding a second-hand pump and a new water flask, he connected them up and soon had me loaded up, this time with two pumps; one that worked, the other that didn't.

Within an hour of getting back, we had water, although the pipes connections had a few leaks because I didn't have the right tools. Something I would tolerate.

Peter was very good to me giving a very large discount and offering to install the in-well pump. I agreed, although I have yet to get this done.

The first few days were a whirlwind of cleaning and sorting out. Moving a large community of soft toys and teddy bears from the room Daryna was using that belonged to my now completely estranged daughter, exploring the home environment, including the summer house, a converted stone chicken shed, which I extended to create a large wood-panelled room with windows that overlooked the river that runs through my land, forming a secure boundary, and the garden, where we used to play badminton.

The house was cold. Being empty, the walls had lost all heat and no matter the radiators and lighting the big fire, the house felt cold. I needed extra radiators and we needed new sim cards for our phone so we headed into Dundalk.

As I installed my new sim card, I got a message through Viber. It was Nataliya, my neighbour in Irpin.

'We are free!'

While we were on our journey, Irpin was attacked and partially occupied by russian forces who had destroyed all the bridges. Anyone who didn't escape at the time Oleg and I had done were trapped and hiding underneath the houses and in bunkers, unable to move until the first evacuation on 4 March, which was limited to women and children by train. This stopped the next day as russian forces attacked the train and bombed the railway bridge to deny people any possibility of escape.

Some very brave women hid in the bakery of a shop and continued cooking bread in secret. They delivered the bread at considerable risk to their lives.

The local Territorial Defence under the leadership of the Mayor, Olexandr Markushin had worked with the Ukraine Armed Forces to fight the russians, but the bombing, artillery and tank attacks were terrible. But we were not to know this yet.

Nataliya, with her husband Sasha and daughter, had escaped over the broken bridge to Kyiv, the one made famous through a photograph of people hiding underneath it.

As I stood in the phone shop, I read her message.

'We are OK, but we couldn't take the old lady who can't walk. She was left with some water, but we haven't food to give her.'

Standing in the Marshes Shopping Centre in Dundalk, a modern stylish building, I was transported back to Irpin. I messaged a friend telling him.

He quickly answered, *'It will be two days before we get there.'*

I understood what he was saying. I knew from Oleg that there was hard fighting, and that the area was infiltrated by russian soldiers. A couple of days later, I was saw a video of where I live and on the corner of the street near the park was the legs and feet of a dead russian. The old woman was freed.

For the next week, I saw more and more the tragedy in Irpin, from friends and neighbours posting on Facebook.

A woman and a child buried at the side of the road, on the green strip separating the footpath from the road. A man buried at the side of the railway near the lake, two bits of wood tied to make a cross. His name and the phone number of the person who buried him in black marker. Small sticks marking the makeshift graves of people in the kindergarten, under trees and in the soft sand of children's play areas.

How can children play there ever again? I wondered.

Only later would I see the massive iron mountains of cars driven by evacuating people, which were attacked and destroyed, either by Tanks or machineguns. Their burned-out frames riddled with bullets. How many people died?

Only later would I see the tank graveyards on small streets I knew so well.

Only later would I see the world's press photographing world leaders, presidents, prime ministers, and senior UN officials standing amid the ruins of houses five minutes from my home.

Only later would I see the dangerous route to freedom Nataliya took, driving makeshift roads across makeshift bridges, through a military landscape of carnage, that I only barely recognised as my neighbourhood.

I saw them first from my Facebook friends who took many photos first, quickly followed by the world's press who plastered every media with words and images I struggled with.

This is my home in Ukraine. My people.

Now in my Irish home, it was the kindness of neighbours. People I hadn't seen in many years, maybe ten or so.

Clare came with clothes and toys for Maria.

Pauline my closest neighbour came to welcome us home. On the last days of our journey, she offered fish soup when we got home. HOME!

I am so grateful for the warmth and love. I can't really show it well. But, thanks!

The 17 March is St Patricks Day and as the chaos of the first few days settled and the house warmed, I decided we should all go and see the parade in Dublin. All except Daryna who was still exhausted. Standing for hours in a massive crowd would be impossible and I wanted to spare her more pain.

We travelled in the morning and finding a gap in the cars near the start of the parade, we walked over.

As we walked, we noticed people with Ukrainian flags. Carrying them, wearing them as cloaks, they were flying from lampposts and the windows of the buildings. But these weren't Ukrainians, they were Irish.

For the first time in history, St Patrick's Day would be dedicated to a country, not Ireland. WOW!

Walking incognito, we stood at the top of O'Connell Street, under Parnell's Monument.

Charles Stewart Parnell made my most favourite statement;

No man has a right to fix the boundary of the march of a nation; no man has a right to say to his country – thus far shalt thou go and no further.

He was speaking with respect to the British occupation in Ireland, directing his comments to the politicians who led that country at the time. I believed it when I first read it as a child. I believe it today. It applies not only to Britain, it applies universally… including russia's war in Ukraine.

Under the statue of this man, we stood, waiting for the parade. Maria on my shoulders, Sofia and Aleksandra decided to explore, only returning after the parade had passed.

As the parade went by, more and more support for Ukraine was shown. People moved aside to let Maria see better and a man gave her an Irish flag to wave.

Between us and the barrier was a family, the parents and two children of about seven and five years old. As we watched, Maria waved and took interest in the bright colours, the bands playing and the cheering of the crowds.

The mother of the children looked and smiled a few times and after thirty minutes said, "I thought I recognised you. Come one, let her down and she can stand with my two girls."

The kindness of strangers once again, this time someone who had seen me on TV, heard me on radio and followed my story.

Parade over, the crowd started to loosen and Sofia and Aleksandra re-appeared. They watched the parade from a different vantage point because it was impossible to return due to the crowds. To be honest, I really didn't think about them as we watched the parade, and they weren't missed by Maria so it was all good.

As we walked down the rapidly thinning crowded O'Connell Street, the presence of Ukrainian flags became more obvious. The street was lined with them. When we got to O'Connell Bridge, we could see four huge flags, each one marking the corners of the bridge. In previous years, these corners were the sole preserve of the Irish flag, but not that day.

For a couple of hours, we wandered Dublin city centre before heading back to the car. Aleksandra had been enraged when Sofia and I went for a walk on our own while Maria and Aleksandra were eating, reminding me that despite a really nice day, the demons that possessed her were far from gone.

Baby Car was hidden in a narrow side street as we approached, I saw two men sitting on the opposite side of the street chatting. As we approached Baby Car, they shouted "*Slava Ukrayini*", which means 'Glory to Ukraine' and is a symbol of Ukrainian sovereignty and resistance.

I shouted back, "*Heroim Slava!*" which means 'Glory to Heroes'; the proper response.

As everyone got in the car, I went over to these men. They were Moldovans who knew Ukraine well. They also knew what russians were doing in their country, which is rarely reported.

Heading home, Sofia reminded me that her brother Mark was coming to Ireland the following day, the 18 March, and we needed to go to Rosslare for three p.m.

"That's OK," I replied.

As we organised our busy breakfast, we had a message from Mark. Then a call from a Polish man.

He had befriended Mark and offered to bring him to Dublin. That was great. Half the distance to travel. So, we went to pick him up, meeting them near the Red Cow Roundabout at seven p.m.

I don't know Mark and Sofia knows little.

He is a brother from another mother, quiet and had not enjoyed much success. Unmarried and never working, he lived with his mother and did jobs for Yura, his brother. Sofia is one of his stepsisters. For me, it was a case of paying Yura back for hosting us in Warsaw and helping Sofia's family.

Mark had come to the wedding but true to form, was very quiet, only being noticed in photographs.

Sofia and I met Mark in the car park, near the Luas stop.

Luas being Dublin's very modern, stylish tram system which criss-crosses the city.

Returning to Omeath in a little over an hour and a half, Mark was given the 'leggedy bed' room. This is a converted stone building next to the house which I renovated and built, with some help from a carpenter.

Originally a cowshed, it had been converted to a garage and I made it into a study, housing my many books, with sofa bed, desk and an ancient settee, a long wooden bench that opens up to make a bed.

I had taken the measurements of the original half hay loft that would have housed the boys of the house, above the cattle for warmth and built a loft, putting a mattress up there to make a bed. Both Svetlana and Ann had used this room and it was handy as a spare room, but perfect for me to chill out and work in quiet, when my children were young.

Mark had these rooms for two reasons. He was a man. There was sensitivity in the 'all girl' remainder of the guests. I was keen to avoid any difficulties, most especially as Iryna, Svetlana's daughter, would come with her friend Nataliya on 23 March, five days later.

Mark had joined his family and I was happy with that. The dynamic was not so peaceful, with him seeking to assert a position for himself that he didn't have, but he did useful chores and cooked for himself.

Unfortunately, he wasn't an experienced cook and managed to burn many things, setting the record for multiple burnings of toast... Twelve times he tried; twelve times he burned, not just one slice, but eight at a time.

In fairness, he scraped the black off and ate the toast, doing so almost ritually.

On the Monday, the 21st, I took Mark down to Morgan's fish factory, a highly respected family-owned fish business fifteen minutes' walk from my house and I asked about a job. We were asked to meet Gerry on Thursday, which we did. Mark started work the following day. Perfect.

During this time, we exorcised the experiences of the journey by tidying, both inside and out.

Sofia dug the vegetable garden and I cut the grass. We both cleared out the greenhouse and I bought new bags of peat and some extra strawberries for the season, to replace those lost when they were left outside for two years.

Sofia bought some seed potatoes and broccoli plants, cauliflower and parsley, planting the potatoes and broccoli outside, where Sofia had dug over. We planted the seeds in seed trays in the greenhouse.

Adding tomatoes to the greenhouse gave us a good base of plants to eat and we were happy to do so.

Sofia loves plants and her mind started to think of her dear orchids and geranium that she nurtured in her apartment in Obolon. There were very many of different colours and she has green fingers, managing to save plants that you would think were gone.

To her delight, Ireland also likes geraniums, and they are sold in many places. This gave Sofia a reason to explore different stores and I was happy that she was taking an interest. Soon, she had a nice collection of colourful plants, in deep reds, pinks, purples and white, buying dark green ceramic pots to add to the ones I already have. Putting them in the porch, Sofia recreated her balcony in Obolon, except for the want of orchids.

A large tree of many branches had fallen in a storm, and I

started to cut it up. I did ask Mark to help, but for some unfathomable reason he decided to cut fruit trees, most especially blackcurrant bushes that yield many kilos of fruit.

When I shouted him to stop, he was shamefaced and upset. Later, he went to rebuild stone walls that sheep had kicked down and helped me trim a bay leaf bush that grew to three metres tall in two years.

The following day, I started the tedious task of cutting the tree of many branches, tedious because of the mass of ivy wrapped round the branches, forming large knots, so big that you could sit inside them like giant nests, when the branches had been upright.

As Mark had demonstrated his wilful incompetence, Sofia and Aleksandra helped pull the cut pieces and put them at the side of the field to provide homes for animals, insects and fungi, while they rotted down over many years.

I had asked Mark to cut the sides of the lane which had become overgrown as I got ready to get Iryna and Nataliya from the airport. He was bored and wanted something to do. I wasn't thinking. Again, his tendencies drew him to cut large branches of a cooking apple tree, instead of the lane, landing him in considerable trouble as he had damaged a heavily fruiting tree that had very tasty apples.

I was fuming. "Stupid boy!" I said more than once.

Taking the tools off him, I asked him to wash the windows outside the house, which were dirty from being unwashed so long.

By the time I was waiting for Iryna and Nataliya, I was reclaiming my composure and I was pleased to see them. I was even more pleased with the tidal wave of positive energy they exuded. They were very happy and a real tour de force of jokes, laughter and warmth.

The regime of registration at Dublin Airport was much more developed than we experienced in Rosslare just two weeks before. In fact, there was a new procedure, including a document, which would be the visa, probably the most comprehensive visa document ever, giving Ukrainians the effective status of an EU citizen, including the right to travel in and out of the country, access to welfare and medical care.

WOW!

When I saw the documents, I spoke with one of the staff from Department of Justice. Yes, I needed to bring the others down to get theirs.

The following day, I brought Daryna, Sofia, Aleksandra and Maria. The day after, Mark.

The procedure was simple, efficient and effective. In a couple of days, we were all good.

Maria had been accepted to the village kindergarten 'Woddlers and Toddlers' even before we had arrived into Ireland. Irene, the superb and ever-dedicated owner of the kindergarten and a very proud Omeathiopian, the name of people from Omeath.

Irene had looked after my own children and her exceptional professionalism had seen her business grow, with a talented and disciplined team of carers and a creative, loving and safe environment for children.

Maria was due to attend, but the day before Aleksandra had been offended and very upset because I had made it clear that she would have to pay towards bills, which she didn't want to do. Nor did she want to stay anywhere else. Essentially, she wanted to be living cost-free, which isn't real life.

Staying in her room for a couple of days, emerging to use

the toilet and cook food, which she ate in her room. Aleksandra would deny Maria to be with anyone else.

Aleksandra had clashed with Mark several times, although Mark was equally to blame as he thought he would have his meals cooked for him and was entitled to eat anything that was in the house, including food that Aleksandra had bought for herself and Maria, which was unacceptable.

Eventually emerging from her self-imposed exile, Aleksandra took an interest in the summer house, another abandoned project of mine.

The summer house was originally a chicken shed at the bottom of the garden, overlooking the river. It consists of two rooms, one smaller than the other.

When I bought the house, it had no doors and the corrugated iron roof was rusted, holes letting water in, but it was mostly dry.

The floor was rough dirt and stones in the larger shed and the concrete floor of the smaller one had holes made by rats biting through.

When my children were small, I had repaired the circular window and a new door was fitted by my former brother-in-law. I kept geese and chickens in the houses for the children's interest, the geese, all twelve of them, forming a fearless gang who would gather around strangers and terrify them.

More than once, the postman threatened to refuse to deliver.

This was my fault. When I bought them as day-old chicks, I made the mistake of keeping them under a lamp in the porch for the first week, as recommended. However, I didn't think, and they imprinted on the porch, and no matter what I did, they would gather around the front door, gaggling, when let. As soon as someone approached, they would hiss and honk.

This was intimidating, but not nearly as much as them flying over from where they were grazing if someone arrived. The sight of large white geese flying towards the porch is impressive, but for visitors, it was pure terror.

Anyway, as the children were older and lost interest in animals, preferring computer games, I decided to modernise the buildings and create a long wooden extension.

My idea was simple. Create a nice stone room with tiled floor as a kitchen and bedroom, use the wooden extension as an outdoor dining room for summer. This is necessary, not only because of Ireland's notorious wet weather in summer, but also due to the hordes of biting insects that plagues you in August, spoiling outside barbecues.

I started the structure while my ex-wife was still at my home, with tensions at their height, and continued after she left, but as the children had no interest, my heart sank, and I lost motivation.

Now, sixteen years later, Aleksandra was enthusiastic and wanted to finish the building, as she saw I had gym equipment in it. Aleksandra persuaded Sofia it would be a great dance and exercise studio.

They busied themselves with cleaning inside and out and Sofia and I painted the inside wall that had been left, half done.

The idea was that we would finish it before Easter, but with Iryna and Nataliya coming, our momentum stalled.

The arrival of the twin tornado that is Iryna and Nataliya broke the tensions as their non-nonsense, funny approach disarmed the relationships. They even took on Daryna, who was struggling to adapt and missed her life in Kyiv. They engaged, empathised, encouraged and explained to each of them that this was temporary and that they were safe.

The stay wasn't long for Iryna and Nataliya, as they returned to Ukraine to be with their boyfriends on 6 April, but their antics, taking Aleksandra under their wing and taking her and Sofia to the pub a few times, enlivened the house and did immense good.

Somewhat predictably, Mark clashed with the girls and became more and more isolated. I was glad he was working but disturbed by his behaviour, as he stayed in the house till after two a.m. as everyone was sleeping. Daryna started to complain that he was walking outside with a torch, which I didn't see, but he did leave the lights of the house on, which was distracting.

In reality, I suspect he was talking on his phone, outside the house so as not to disturb anyone, but obviously, he attracted Daryna's attention.

It was time I spoke with him about finding somewhere else to live, but before I had a chance, he beat me to it.

On the 10th, Mark left without any notice or thank you, taking his belongings. Everyone was surprised at the suddenness but were happy he made the right decision.

I haven't heard from him since, but as far as I know he is still working at the fish factory. I have to say I was relieved, as once the girls had left, Aleksandra's anger issues, which had disappeared, returned with full force. Had Mark been around, he would have been the target of abuse and I wouldn't wish that on him.

The next two weeks though were relatively calm. Sofia was struggling with the stress and emotional upheaval and Aleksandra was very helpful to her. The problem seemed to be her relationship with Daryna, whose own emotions meant she would say things that were best ignored, but that isn't Aleksandra's character.

The four of us managed to find a balance for Easter, which was on 23 April and was good. Aleksandra even cooked Paska, tall round tower of bread with raisins and dried orange rind, topped off with icing. She even coloured eggs.

I cooked Turkey and roast vegetables, which was well received. I was hoping for normality, but the clashes with Daryna continued.

Our wonderful neighbour, Pauline, who had welcomed us home when we first arrived, dropped over with a tasty pineapple sponge cake, which completed our feast.

After Easter, Aleksandra and Sofia were ready for jobs and I agreed to take them to see people in Carlingford.

We went into one hotel and the owner was pleased to see us. He called over the chef to discuss possible openings and he recognised me, again from the TV.

The discussion was lengthy and very positive, Aleksandra could have a trial the following day.

When we went out, I said we would go with Sofia to find her work, but Aleksandra wasn't happy. She wanted to walk around Carlingford with Sofia and relax. She asked me to go back and look after Maria. I refused.

Causing a scandal in the street isn't something I condone, so I said I would take them back and return with Sofia.

Dropping off Aleksandra, we returned, leaving the CVs, meeting people who recognised me and generally being well-met in the warm spring sun.

The next four days were telling.

Aleksandra demanded to know who would drive her to the job in the morning and I said, with her aggressive tone, no one would. She became enraged. I was indifferent. No one would talk like that in my presence and get satisfaction. There was a bus that left Omeath to Carlingford and it took ten minutes.

Aleksandra demanded to be driven. It didn't suit her to go by bus.

I said no.

The next four days saw Aleksandra holed up in her room with Maria, blankets and coats blocking the food and window, so it must have been dark.

All the food from the fridge, freezer and cool store belonging to Aleksandra was taken up to the room, including raw meat, fish eggs, etc. Other than going to the toilet, she didn't emerge, nor did Maria.

The atmosphere was one of stress... I kept calm and projected comfort and normalcy to Daryna and Sofia, hoping this deep cloud would not break into another aggressive storm.

Sofia had managed to find a job and that helped to distract her, but not Daryna.

On the Sunday, I found Daryna collapsed and unresponsive on the floor of the living room. I called Aleksandra five times, but no answer.

Calling the emergency services, I followed the direction from the operator on the phone.

Tilt her head, remove false teeth, count her breathing out loud.

It took forever for the ambulance to arrive and while I waited, Daryna's breathing quickened, faulted and became shallow and stopped. Then started again, then stopped. Then started; each time, her breathing being slower and weaker than before. Her colourless face was pained, but she was silent. No noise, other than her breathing. Time expanded into an eternity.

On several occasions, I demanded of Daryna not to die. Exactly like in a film. Not here, not now, not after this... but there was no response, no word, movement, nothing. Daryna was dying,

The relief I felt when the ambulance crew arrived was minimal as they were asking questions, wanting information, getting me to write contact details, name, PPSN number etc. Highly efficient, they worked on Daryna, cutting her new coat and top off. Her recently acquired favourite clothes. There was no other way, but I knew she would be unhappy about this.

Sofia was at work at this time.

With the commotion, Aleksandra came downstairs and angrily demanded why I didn't call her, making accusations. I replied that I called her five times and the crew looked at her. Aleksandra wanted scandal, but instead started loudly crying and shouting at Daryna who was unconscious.

As the crew cut off her clothes and brought in resuscitation equipment, Aleksandra stood over them wailing loudly, but not tearfully. I was busy getting things.

An ambulance support car arrived as I was at the ambulance, fetching something asked for. I am sure they did this to get me away from the scene, allowing them to engage Aleksandra with questions and tasks.

Soon, Daryna was in the ambulance with the door shut, as they worked to try stabilising her after having a seizure whilst inside. Aleksandra was standing outside with an intense look on her face, angry and upset in equal measure, often shouting, but I have no idea what she was saying and it was incoherent and I had other things to organise and was trying to call Sofia and warn her.

It was fifteen minutes later that Sofia arrived from work. She immediately understood what was going on and went to get more details, calmly, purposefully and focused. As the direct relation, Sofia had to give her details and Daryna's medical history, which I didn't know.

Then we were told to follow the ambulance as it took Daryna to hospital. "Don't try to keep up. We will be driving fast with sirens on. She is very sick, and we don't have much time."

"OK," I replied.

We left for the hospital ten minutes later, having collected all we needed.

At the hospital, we were shown to a room with religious paraphernalia and told to wait.

Aleksandra and Maria waited near the door, we waited at the other end of the room. No words were spoken between us, and Maria was commanded to stay with Aleksandra also. Apparently, we are bad people, according to Aleksandra.

Over eight hours later, the doctors visited us three times to ask questions and give results of tests. They wanted to build up a picture of Daryna's health.

They asked Sofia to sit with Daryna for a short time to explain that she was in hospital, after which Aleksandra demanded to go, taking Maria.

The doctor explained that children were not allowed in intensive care, angering Aleksandra who demanded to be let in. The doctor said no.

Increasingly visibly angry, Aleksandra asked again. He said he would check. Thirty minutes later, he came back and said no.

After another thirty minutes, a nurse came and suggested

Aleksandra and Maria stay in another room, next to the one we were in, it having been vacated, which they did, much to my relief as her pressure cooker mood was being triggered each time anyone spoke with Sofia or me. She was equally insistent that Maria didn't come to us or even look in our direction.

Each time we passed the open door of the room she was in, Aleksandra glowered.

Later, the doctor came and explained that Daryna was very sick. He said it would not be possible to resuscitate her if she needed it because of her age and fragility, asking Sofia if she agreed. Sofia understood but couldn't answer. He accepted the silence as acceptance and returned to Daryna, giving her morphine.

Thirty minutes later, the nurse asked Sofia to sit with Daryna for a while and after a while, I went to buy a sandwich for Sofia.

It took about thirty minutes to get refreshments as it was Sunday evening and only a fuel station was open. I was glad of the fresh air and the walk.

Returning, Sofia came out and ate the food and drank the coffee I bought.

Forty minutes later, Sofia asked me to speak with the doctor as she didn't want to sit by the bedside. Too stressful and in any case Daryna was unconscious.

The doctor was happy that Daryna was stable, and said they were prepping her to go to the ward, but he said the situation wasn't good, and it was uncertain whether she would last the night.

We left, Aleksandra and Maria silent, immediately locking themselves in their room again when we returned home.

We waited for bad news... It was coming.

In the next three days, Aleksandra was with Maria in her room and never once asked how Daryna was. Not once.

On the Monday, I called the hospital for an update and see about visiting. Daryna was in the severe stroke ward and was stable, but that she was very sick.

There was no possibility of visiting, everything was being done, tests were being taken and we could call again the following day to see what was possible.

At around noon, we had a call from the hospital asking us to come down in thirty minutes. That was impossible, as it takes forty-five minutes as a minimum. We agreed to be there at 14.30 as the doctor treating Daryna wanted lunch.

So, we arrived.

Daryna was on the 9th floor and in bed when we were allowed into the locked ward. Weak but happy to see us, her arms deep purple and brown with bruises, intravenous drips on both arms and monitors beeping.

We were welcomed by the nurse who went to fetch the doctor, an Irish woman, clearly in command of the situation.

Daryna had a seizure, but she had damage from strokes which occurred in the past. It's possible they are very old. She was weak and vulnerable, most likely due to the journey and any stress she had experienced.

Sofia was surprised. There was never an indication of a stroke.

The doctor went on to say that there will be more tests, including an MRI and we needed to help explain to Daryna what she should do when she went into the machine.

The doctor asked again about recent medical history, but said there was no long-term damage done.

229

Then she said, "There can't be stress in Daryna's life. It could do harm, serious harm." As she spoke, I heard the word death. If Daryna was stressed, she could die.

Leaving us, we stayed awhile, pleased that Daryna seemed OK and certainly in good hands.

When we got home, Aleksandra and Maria were in their room.

Later that night, I told Sofia that Aleksandra's anger was a risk and it can't be allowed to continue. Sofia agreed.

The die was cast.

To my surprise, Aleksandra emerged with Maria the next morning, shortly after Sofia left for work.

"I want a key to the house. We are going out and will not come back till late," Aleksandra said, demanding and unpleasant.

Here was my cue.

"Aleksandra, I hope you are looking for somewhere else to stay."

With that, Aleksandra started demanding a key with menace.

I said, "Sorry, Aleksandra, you can't stay here. Your anger is harming people."

As she insisted on a key, I repeated this three times, each time to an increasingly aggressive Aleksandra.

Taking and trying keys that didn't fit, Aleksandra became more agitated and then said she would destroy everything in the house. Break everything...everything, her eyes burned, staring and unseeing.

Calmly, I said no. She would have no key and she needed to find somewhere new.

She took my laptop and phones and started wandering, her

eyes staring but not seeing. Walking on tip-toes, bouncing, saying she would stay as long as she wanted and made threats about Sofia and me, which I am certain she meant. Probably still does, to be honest.

I told her I would call the guards.

As she became even more demanding and threatening to crash the devices into the ground, I called 999 in full view of Aleksandra who could hear exactly what I said.

She put the devices down and took Maria, who had been a silent witness to this, back into her room.

The guards came twenty minutes later and as they spoke with me, they could hear Aleksandra screaming, ranting and throwing things in her room. She was calling several people and roaring down the phone. One of them was Sofia.

As the guards took notes, the noise began to lessen and one of them ventured up to her room, while the other stayed with me and went through a standard Domestic Incident Report form.

We were downstairs but could hear the calm voice of the guard and Aleksandra's insistent loud voice. I could hear her make claims about me, none of which were true.

After completing the forms, the second guard joined their colleague upstairs and spoke with Aleksandra, who was becoming quieter.

After fifteen minutes, they came downstairs and said she was calmer now. They asked me to call if there were more problems and left.

Twenty-four hours later, just as Sofia returned from work, an old red car arrived at the house and Aleksandra took all her things, with Maria, and left in an unknown direction. No thank you, nothing, other than anger when she demanded I open my car to let her get one of Maria's books. Ahh, well!

Shortly after, the guards arrived for a follow-up call and give me the contact details of the Irish Red Cross, to help find Aleksandra an alternative place to live.

They checked that the room was empty and took Aleksandra's contact details so they could speak with her and ensure her safety. I was mighty pleased with their professionalism and thoroughness.

As I apologised for the trouble and made my profound gratitude known, they sympathetically smiled and said, domestic calls are eighty per cent of their job. God help them.

Silence returned to the house, and I could feel Sofia's pain, losing Maria on top of worries about Daryna was hard.

Later that day, I spoke with Sofia over a hot cup of tea. She was upset.

I explained that in Ireland, it's not easy to disappear and wherever they were, they were being supervised. That would not be the case had it happened in Ukraine. They would have simply been untraceable.

All the same, it was hard. Very hard.

And I was a bad man. Well, in my eyes I was.

But it was either Daryna's life or Aleksandra and Maria in an uncertain relationship for an unknowable length of time. Death is permanent and forgiveness impossible. I did my job.

A few weeks later, they had moved again and were living in a hotel, proclaiming that they were happy.

No one died. Well, not yet.

Chapter 15
Heartbreak

And so, we come to the last chapter, well, the last chapter for now. Stories may end, but life goes on, but what happens can't be known, nor written about. Not yet.

But, ninety-seven days from the start of this extended war from 2014, there are conclusions to be drawn, because people are dead, injured, raped and devastated by loss. Not only loss of family and friends, but of homes, mementos and meaning.

To write about heartbreak is to describe the layers of an onion and I will start from the outside in.

Almost eighty years after World War II, the system of checks, balances and securities have been shattered. The guarantee which Ukraine was provided in the Budapest Memorandum, leading to nuclear disarmament, has been broken by one of its guarantors, russia. But that was in 2014. The other guarantors did nothing, laying the ground for the current phase of war.

Violations of the Geneva Convention exceed over ten thousand and counting. The use of banned weapons continues on a daily basis, with no mechanism to hold russia to account. This Convention is dead.

The United Nations Security Council, designed to avoid such conflicts, was chaired by russia during this aggression and is entirely emasculated and unfit for purpose.

The EU is dominated by corruption, greed and self-interest, most notably the founding countries of Germany and France, along with Russophiles in Hungary, Austria, Italy and elsewhere.

The International Red Cross has failed over a million people deported under force of arms from Ukraine to remote parts of russia. Their treatment and fates hidden from the world. Many of these 'evacuations' have been overseen by the IRC. Witnesses on the train station, can you imagine that?

Under pressure to sustain relationships, countries more willing to support Ukraine's cause have been restrained and hesitant in the supply of weapons and materiel. The delays have cost lives, incurred damage and increased exposure to atrocities and abuse of human rights.

The heartbreak comes from failures to realise consequences, which extend beyond Ukraine, to world food shortages, projections of millions of dead by famine, ecological disaster from pollution in the Azov and Black seas, where we explored and potentially beyond, to the Mediterranean.

The heartbreak also comes from a more dangerous future, with russia threatening other countries with the same and worse.

Sadly, the young and unborn generations face a world far less secure, because of the failings of a generation now in their 50s, 60s and 70s. People who lived in the rubble of World War II have condemned children to a life less secure. Those that we entrust our safety are now the greatest risk to that safety, through corruption, cowardice and selfish interest.

Heart-breaking.

The second layer comprises the people of Irpin, Bucha,

Hostomel and Vorzel, my neighbours and community.

It was 4 March when women and children had the first opportunity to evacuate, but the russian forces bombed the train on the second day; they bombed the railway bridges, preventing trains escaping.

Evacuations were done under gunfire and many people were killed trying to escape. Shot in their cars, on bikes, and on foot. The boy who was always seen carrying his football, when he wasn't having a kickabout in the back of the houses, shot in the back. Dead. For fear he would tell others he saw russian soldiers. Cold, callous and inhuman.

Many people, including Oleg's neighbour, who didn't leave when Oleg did and was captured trying to escape, tortured and shot. His body being left at the side of the road. A woman and her son shot and buried at the side of a car park. Another mother and child buried in the soft sand of a children's play area, marked with sticks. A man killed and buried next to the railway line, sticks used as a marker, his name and phone number written in black marker for his relatives to find him.

People hiding in the underground shelters of high-rise buildings, houses and garages starved and went without water and medicines. People who went to supply them were killed. The Chief of Medicine Dr Anton Dovgopol held at gunpoint, prevented from treating people and made to bury sixty-seven civilians himself. The hospitals shelled by tanks and artillery fire.

Lyudmila Pershin, a tireless worker who delivered aid and information throughout the occupation, lost her husband, who was killed in battle.

Women hiding with their children were surrounded by russian tanks. The soldiers taking it in turns raping them until

Ukrainian forces caused them to flee.

Houses looted and violated, tonnes of stolen items taken to Belarus, then posted to cities across russia, as loot, leaving families heartbroken at the trashed scenes of personal belongings, strewn, used as a toilet, violated and vandalised.

Homes bombed, burned and destroyed with armoured vehicles crashing through them.

The city square was attacked, the library being just one focus of attention. The famous Chestnut store, with its iconic clock tower and traditional wares gutted, erased from the streetscape, entirely gone.

Pokrovska park was bombed, trees stripped of their branches. The Avenue of the Heroes opposite the park, dedicated to those who defended Ukraine after 2014, shot to pieces. Kamelot destroyed, leaving a blackened skeleton of a building.

The Conference Centre at the bottom of Pokrovska Street, where the buses from Obolon stopped, attacked and badly damaged.

The nearby school which catered for over a thousand pupils, destroyed, along with the kindergartens in many places.

The shopping centre, 'White House', and the new shops selling fresh fish and meat, which opened only six months ago, destroyed. The small bridge connecting Irpin to the Kyiv Road, destroyed.

Antonov's Mryia, the world's largest plane and Hostomel airport, totally destroyed.

The lakes weren't spared. Dead fish and other animals created a biohazard, hundreds of shells in the water making it unsafe. The water polluted.

The forests are unsafe due to unexploded bombs and

shells, booby traps and pollution from destroyed machines and ammunition.

My neighbours' houses were bombed and burned out. Nadiya Kolomiets, who taught me Ukrainian and helped with my wedding speech, her home destroyed, only demolition awaits.

My home was bombed and fired upon with automatic weapons mounted on a tank, smashing eighteen double glazed windows and making holes in the steel frame of the balcony. The roof is now open to the elements as full roof sheets were destroyed. Rain seeps into my apartment, creating corrosive damage and brown marks on the newly plastered ceilings.

Irpin, which in February was home to seventy five thouand people now has less than twenty five thousand and cannot sustain them, despite the clean-up and the creation of a temporary, modular shelter complex.

But the clean-up and rehabilitation is starting and planning to create Irpin as a smart, sustainable city has attracted the attention of specialists from across the world, including one hundred and twenty architects from Ukraine, internationally renowned town and disaster recovery planners from Spain, Chile and elsewhere, and world leaders in politics and institutions.

For example, many prime ministers and presidents of countries across Europe have visited Irpin in recent weeks.

Prime Minister of Canada, Justin Trudeau, Prime Minister of Finland Sana Marin, Dr Tedros Adhanom Ghebreyesus, Director General of the World Health Organisation and many others stood, stared and walked not ten mins from my home in Irpin, making promises that need to be kept.

There are positive signs, as the EU shutters ninety per cent of oil purchases from russia which funds the war and nation states terminate gas contracts, further denying money. Sanctions on technology degrades its ability to replace weapons, while thirty one thousand Russian fighters are dead.

On the family front, Daryna greatly missed her home and her friends before she became ill. Being in a foreign country without being able to speak the language or drive, poses distinct challenges, fear of isolation and loneliness.

But, Daryna was released on the Friday, the day after Aleksandra left with Maria, and five days after the seizure. It wasn't a stroke, and she was with me when she had it.

Had she been in Kyiv, where she lives alone, it could have been days before she was found and, during war, neither ambulances nor medical treatments are easily available when needed. Certainly, the medicines and technology used to save her life in an Irish hospital would not be readily available in Kyiv.

But now she is lively, watches her favourite TV programmes on a smart TV we bought for her, sits in the sun, sheltered by the large, glazed porch, with her dog Lisa, and calls her friends. Calling at least four of them every single day, chatting, gossiping and laughing.

Daryna cooks for herself and eats well, takes her medicine, jokes, and moves niftily enough for an eighty year old, only being achy after her four-hour shopping trips to Dundalk, where she inspects everything, without fail, and buys what she needs with money from the Irish government, which is eight times greater than what she was given in Ukraine, as a pensioner.

There is no doubt that Sofia is upset at the loss of her granddaughter and no words can take away a pain like that.

There is also no question that she is torn by memories of a life lived and the pull of friends who repeatedly ask her to return to Kyiv. Her isolation from me as she thinks deeply is to be accepted and her decisions respected.

But she is driving alone by herself on Ireland's country roads (something she would not do in Kyiv), working and getting more money than from her job in Kyiv. She is free to travel across Europe and learn about a new culture, while improving her English, which is already very good, and exploring Ireland, already visiting Donegal, the Cliffs of Moher, Galway and Dublin.

As we venture through life, we all must pass from one stage to another. This is where Sofia is at, unsure whether to do it in Kyiv or in the Cooley Mountains and the townland of Tullaghomeath. Who am I to say what is best? No one.

And what about me?

I was born and raised into a cool, friendly, kind and intelligent family who has inspired more than they disappoint (maybe I am adopted?).

It is my family who provide money to cover the next few months' costs, as I sort my life out, devastated both financially and career-wise.

But I am named after St Brendan the traveller. My last name means 'Sea-Warrior', I have lived my life with adventures of the mind and the body, both in business and in geography.

Like always, my nose will lead my face into a future of opportunities of my own making and from the kindness of strangers. Whether there be storms, tempests or welcoming winds, I will venture on.

The people have risen. Success is a matter of application,

persistence and time. russia will be beaten.

If we meet on the road… you will be well met, that's for sure, as long as your moral compass points in the right direction.

So, heartbreak?

Yes, certainly… but in the memory of others we venture onward, certain that the kindness of strangers is in abundance, when you're in need.

Our story is testament to that.

Be brave.

Slava Ukrayini!

Glóir don Úcráin!